California Studies in Food and Culture

Darra Goldstein, Editor

M. F. K. Fisher
among the Pots and Pans

M. F. K. Fisher
among the Pots and Pans

Celebrating Her Kitchens

Joan Reardon

Foreword by Amanda Hesser

University of California Press   *Berkeley   Los Angeles   London*

University of California Press, one of the most distinguished
university presses in the United States, enriches lives around the
world by advancing scholarship in the humanities, social sciences,
and natural sciences. Its activities are supported by the UC Press
Foundation and by philanthropic contributions from individuals
and institutions. For more information, visit www.ucpress.edu.

University of California Press
Berkeley and Los Angeles, California

University of California Press, Ltd.
London, England

© 2008 by Joan Reardon

Frontispiece. Portrait 1984, copyright George Hurrell, courtesy of the
Estate of George Hurrell. George Hurrell is a registered trademark.
All photographs unless otherwise noted in the captions are from
the collection of Kennedy Friede Golden.
Watercolors are by Avram Dumitrescu.

Library of Congress Cataloging-in-Publication Data
Reardon, Joan, 1930–
    M. F. K. Fisher among the pots and pans : celebrating her kitchens /
Joan Reardon ; foreword by Amanda Hesser.
    p. cm. — (California studies in food and culture ; 22)
    Includes bibliographic references.
    ISBN 978-0-520-25555-5 (cloth : alk. paper)
    1. Fisher, M. F. K. (Mary Frances Kennedy), 1908–1992.   2. Food
writers—United States—Biography.   3. Cookery. I. Title.
TX649.F5R428   2008
641.5092—dc22
[B]   2008002163

Manufactured in Canada
17 16 15 14 13 12 11 10 09 08
10 9 8 7 6 5 4 3 2 1

For Mary Frances
in honor of the hundredth anniversary
of her birth, July 3, 2008

Contents

Foreword

Amanda Hesser

Of all the lush food descriptions in M. F. K. Fisher's writing, the one that remains most vivid in my mind is that of the tangerines that Fisher once roasted on her radiator and then chilled on the windowsill in her pension in Strasbourg.

"Peel them gently," she instructed.

Do not bruise them, as you watch soldiers pour past and past the corner and over the canal towards the watched Rhine. Separate each plump little pregnant crescent. If you find the Kiss, the secret section, save it for Al.

After you have put the pieces of tangerine on the paper on the hot radiator, it is best to forget about them. . . . On the radiator the sections of tangerines have grown even plumper, hot and full. You carry them to the window, pull it open, and leave them for a few minutes on the packed snow of the sill. They are ready.

. . . I cannot tell you why they are so magical. Perhaps it is that little shell, thin as one layer of enamel on a Chinese bowl, that crackles so tinily, so ultimately under your teeth. Or the rush of cold pulp just after it. Or the perfume. I cannot tell.

Fisher's entire relationship to cooking and writing and eating is contained in these few short paragraphs. On display is her relish of the pleasures of eating, her extraordinary alertness, and most notably her trademark casualness about homemaking and cooking. There were no thoroughly equipped kitchens or lavish meals in her realm. If her radiator had to serve as a stove, so it would.

Throughout her adult life, Fisher seemed to yearn not for the comforts and order of her upper-middle-class upbringing in Whittier, California, but for the challenges of settling into a new home. Though we like to think of Fisher in three settings—growing up in Whittier, then abroad in France and Switzerland, and finally, in her later years, at Last House on the Bouverie Ranch in Glen Ellen, California—she was actually a vagabond. While she occasionally had reasons to relocate—divorces, family illness, the Depression—Fisher was restless and moved with alarming frequency, living in more than twenty places in all. In Provence alone, where she lived five times, twice with her daughters, Anne and Kennedy, and three times with her sister Norah, she stayed in at least a handful of homes.

I've often had the impression that she reveled in the hardships of a place. Only a few times in her life did she have a kitchen with four walls. And when a kitchen was too small to contain the food she would cook in it, she acted like a poet who must jacket herself into the constraints of a sonnet, and would make still lifes of fruits and vegetables, setting them on tables and windowsills, letting her kitchen expand, if not physically then psychically, into other parts of the house.

Not all of Fisher's kitchens were undesirable, as Joan Reardon notes in her careful and revealing examination. In the one at Le Paquis in Switzerland, where she lived with Dillwyn Parrish during what was probably the happiest period of her life, there was lots of light, a stove, room for hanging pots and pans, even a root cellar. "In winter, the couple entertained in front of the fireplace," Reardon writes, "and invited their guests to serve themselves from the large casserole simmering on the stove and from the salad bowl dominating the sideboard." But more often than not, Fisher's kitchens were spare, ragtag affairs. One was so cold, she had to dress in a fur coat and gloves to cook in it.

Fisher had a fondness for improvisation, which, along with her affection for inadequate workspaces, is a quality found surprisingly often in great food writers. When Elizabeth David was growing up, her nanny would often use the nursery hearth fire to soften gooseberries in sugar and to warm mushrooms, gathered from a nearby field, in cream. David once wrote in the Smallbone of Devizes' catalogue that "what you can cook on a stove in a passage or on a staircase landing, or over a gas ring or small open fire, is fairly surprising. Granted, the will to do it, plus a spirit of enterprise and a little imagination, are necessary elements in learning to cook. You have to have a healthy appetite, too, and not worry too much over the failures or shortcomings of your kitchen and its equipment." After the war, one of David's kitchens had a table that covered the bath: she had to clear the table and remove it from its perch to bathe. Likewise, Laurie Colwin once had a tiny apartment kitchen with no sink. She did the dishes in her bathtub and dried them on a rack set over her toilet.

But Fisher chose to cook in so many different poorly appointed kitchens, across so many years, that her galley slaving seems a conscious choice. In part it was surely a self-denial born of her tame, disciplined WASP upbringing, but I suspect she was also doing penance for her rebellious sensualism, corseting her desires.

Then, too, not having a refrigerator or an oven also has certain practical benefits. It built in parameters for Fisher's meals. Without an oven you cannot bake cakes and many desserts. With one burner, you are limited to a single cooked dish. And if you only have a few plates, how many courses can visitors expect? Her tiny kitchens streamlined her menus and created the conditions for heroic accomplishment: praise is always given to those who can produce a decent meal from a single burner.

She cooked with a survivalist's economy, a style her older daughter, Anne Parrish, called "unfashionably simple and good." She would often prepare one cooked dish and a salad and accompany them with roasted chickens, bread, and dessert, all bought at the store—a smoke and mirrors feast.

Most cooks would find themselves in tears without a working stove, but Fisher embraced her circumstances with enthusiasm and fortitude. In *The Gastronomical Me*, she wrote fondly of cooking in her apartment in Dijon, shortly after she was married to Al Fisher: "It was the first real day-to-day meal-after-meal cooking I'd ever done, and was only a little less complicated than performing an appendectomy on a life-raft, but after I got used to hauling water and putting together three courses on a table the size of a bandana and lighting the portable oven without blowing myself clear into the living room instead of only halfway, it was fun."

There is a lesson in this for us now: today's kitchens have become palaces of aspiration. They are so enormous that they occasion both infinite possibility and unattainable expectation. There is promise in a second dishwasher—the promise of large parties. And there is melancholy in its disuse.

Anthony Bourdain wrote that "food respects confidence, and abhors uncertainty." Fisher might not have thought much of Bourdain and his bluntly gritty views on food and cooking, but she would have grasped his point instantly, as we do when we read her. Never was something as plain as a tangerine treated with such confidence, such utter certainty. A kitchen is just a small place to think about food.

Introduction

M. F. K. Fisher liked holidays, anniversaries, and, especially, birthdays. She frequently celebrated her own birthday from July 3 through July 14, Bastille Day, the day her grandmother and namesake had been born. During her childhood and school years, a special cake, menu, or event usually marked her actual birthday, the third of July. Traditional Independence Day fireworks followed the day after, and she liked to think of them as another special gift. As an adult, Mary Frances received imaginative birthday presents from her three husbands—a sonnet from Al, a painting from Dillwyn, an antique pin from Donald—and thoughtful gifts from her daughters, usually painstakingly made by hand. And in her middle years, she celebrated many birthdays at her favorite restaurants in Marseille and Aix.

Toward the end of her long career, friends, fans, and readers made her birthdays very special occasions. To honor her seventieth birthday, Alice Waters planned a memorable dinner at Chez Panisse with courses inspired by the titles of her books. For Fisher's eightieth birthday, guests gathered at a $100-a-plate dinner at a San Francisco Bay Area restaurant, where Craig Claiborne referred to Fisher as "a national treasure," and Robert Mondavi toasted her, saying, "You've raised the image of food and wine in this country." This eightieth-birthday celebration was followed by another on July 6 at the San Francisco Public Library, and a few months later there was yet another gala at the Herbst Theatre.

July 3, 2008, marks the hundredth anniversary of M.F.K. Fisher's birth, and the centennial offers another occasion for special dinners and tributes and, one hopes, an opportunity to look more closely at some of the less-explored aspects of her works and days. To this end, in *M.F.K. Fisher among the Pots and Pans* I have focused on her self-defined role as a cook, revisited her many kitchens, and reconsidered her recipes, which have all too often been regarded as afterthoughts and embellishments rather than signposts along the way of her life.

The idea for this book evolved from Amanda Hesser's tribute in the fiftieth-anniversary edition of *The Art of Eating*, in which Hesser observed that "there is one place where I have never felt quite as if I could peer over [Fisher's] shoulder, or listen to her thoughts and worries: the kitchen." After reviewing some of Fisher's most memorable stories about food and finding few answers to the sorts of questions "that obsess today's food lovers," Hesser concluded, "for me, her life as a cook will always feel like a missing piece."

Because critics and admirers have emphasized Fisher the writer, cosmopolitan traveler, and gastronomic philosopher, her role as a cook and kitchen habitué, as well as the symbiotic relationship between the kitchen and dining room that evolved over the course of her life, have been neglected. Fortunately, her words lead the way. "Anything can be a lodestar in a person's life, I suppose, and for some fortunates like me, the kitchen serves well," Fisher wrote in her pitch-perfect essay "Two Kitchens in Provence." "Often the real influence of a lodestar is half understood, or partly unsuspected, but with a little reflection it grows clear to me that kitchens have always played a mysterious part in my shaping."

Commenting on her childhood, she wrote, "A kitchen, the *kitchen*, was indeed intrinsic to family living when I grew up. The first one I remember was a dismal, dark, unventilated but roomy hole. . . . But it always smelled fine, with countless good dishes. I never felt unwelcome there. Later, kitchens became brighter and simpler and smaller, as I grew up and then coped with my own in many places. But always they had wonderful smells and a warm rich welcome, and as I matured I came to understand the mystique or whatever it may be called, of sitting again in that room, talking and listening and nibbling."

Her affinity to that special, nurturing place, moreover, has always been evident in her writing, and she introduced many people—Anita, Ora, the McLure sisters, and other housekeepers—who were recalled, sometimes renamed, and often reconfigured in a domestic setting. She also re-created the sights, smells, sounds, and tastes of her childhood kitchens. Her recipes, especially, reflected the apprenticeship she had served in the Whittier kitchens as well as the wit and wisdom she had acquired over the years by reading Auguste Escoffier, Isabella Beeton, Marion Harland, Irma Rombauer, and Julia Child. And the simple dishes she prepared in her kitchens, whether those kitchens were makeshift or well appointed, embodied her individual approach to celebrating the pleasures of the table and to vesting food with an overlay of metaphoric meaning.

To revisit the kitchens that influenced Fisher—to consider the dishes she prepared and ate, to notice the range of foods and marketplaces she encountered in the many places she lived, to appreciate the ambience of the meals she savored alone, *à deux*, or with a few chosen diners—is also to revisit almost a century of change in the cooking and eating patterns of the United States and of Fisher's adopted country, France. From the first decades of the twentieth century, when domestic help was commonly available to middle- and upper-class Americans, to the dawn of our national obsession with all things culinary, Fisher lived through a remarkable period in the history of food.

For those who do not know the significance of Fisher's work, I hope that *M. F. K. Fisher among the Pots and Pans* will be an introduction to the woman who has been a singular voice in gastronomical writing since the publication of her first book, *Serve It Forth*, in 1937. In that book, Fisher explored the pleasures of the table and culinary lore from cookbooks as old as *Apicius de re Coquinaria* (circa 25 BC–79 AD) and as influential as *Mrs. Beeton's Book of Household Management* (1861) and included essays on topics ranging from childhood indulgences to the social status of vegetables. During the 1940s, Fisher's most productive period, she published four additional books about dining and food, which were gathered together in 1954 under the title *The Art of Eating: The Collected Gastronomical Works of M. F. K. Fisher*. With that collection, and with her brilliant translation of Brillat-Savarin's *Physiology of Taste*, she not only secured her reputation as a writer but also began to change the focus of culinary writing in America. Adopting a style and approach unlike that of earlier American gastronomers—George Wechsberg, Alexis Licine, Lucius Beebe, and A. J. Liebling—and departing from the pattern established by food journalists—who wrote about nutrition, balanced meals, and entertaining—Fisher wrote about the art of eating and drinking with intelligence and grace, and wove autobiography, nostalgia, and incidents from culinary history into essays so distinctive that they contributed to a new genre of food literature.

In addition to more than twenty books published between 1937 and her death in 1992, Fisher contributed articles to *Coronet*, *House Beautiful*, and *Gourmet* in the 1940s and to the *New Yorker* in the 1960s and 1970s. She also frequently wrote for *Vogue*, *Westways*, *Ladies' Home Journal*, *Atlantic Monthly*, *Esquire*, and *Holiday*. When Fisher contributed to Time-Life's *The Cooking of Provincial France* in 1968, she became actively associated with such rising culinary stars as James Beard, Julia Child, Judith Jones, and Craig Claiborne. After North Point Press reissued many of her books in the 1980s, Fisher received still more recognition and honors, including election to the American Academy of Arts and Letters in 1991. With many of her books in continuous print, her name is identified with a tradition of culinary writing marked by excellence.

The sources for this tribute to M. F. K. Fisher are varied and many. First and foremost are Fisher's *How to Cook a Wolf* (1942), *An Alphabet for Gourmets* (1949), and *With Bold Knife and Fork* (1969). A close reading of the latter has been particularly rewarding, and now I understand more fully the fondness Fisher's younger daughter has for this book. But to write about Fisher is also to reference many of her other books, especially *The Art of Eating* and her illuminating accounts of living abroad.

During the course of researching Fisher's biography, I also read more than two hundred of her published magazine articles and became familiar with many of her yearly appointment books, where she took note of the meals she served, the diets she tried, and the ideas she had for recipes. All of this material was extremely helpful in re-creating and updating the recipes included in this book, although there was still a great deal of reconstructive work to make the recipes easy to use for those cooks accustomed to detailed instructions. In some instances, the list of ingredients for a recipe was incomplete; in other cases, the recipe instructions were truncated or simply implied. Each of the recipes, however, represents an important aspect of Fisher's life from her earliest years to the home she called "Last House," and together they reflect the food preferences she had in childhood, the role of French cuisine in her evolution as a cook, the influence of California's agricultural abundance on her seasonal table, and the impact of her work as a writer for food journals and magazines. Often thought of as illustrations by her critics and readers, or, as she wrote in the preface to *Serve It Forth*, as "birds in a tree—if there is a comfortable branch," Fisher's recipes have attracted less attention than her prose, but they should not be overlooked. Writing about Fisher and her recipes in the *Los Angeles Times*, Ruth Reichl noted, "When we began cooking these recipes in our Test Kitchen, we found that every single one of them was absolutely wonderful."

Having been a guest at Last House for extended periods in 1987 and 1988, I came to know Fisher as a storyteller, a woman of strongly held opinions, and a generous hostess. She liked to say that the incidents that she wrote about and often repeated had been carefully stored in her memory, but she never missed an opportunity to spice up a good tale, and she had little or no regard for the factual accuracy of her narratives, which often surprised and even embarrassed her family and friends. With an astonishing frequency she recounted events and anecdotes in a magazine article, only to repeat them—with slight variation—in a book. She could also be prickly about her name and insisted that visitors address her as "Mary Frances." She had no tolerance for the shortened "M. F. K." or for what she termed the "feminist" insistence on "Fisher," and her preferences greatly influenced my decision to refer to her using her preferred name, "Mary Frances," in this intimate portrait of her in her various kitchens.

During my visits with Fisher I also had firsthand experience with her innate hospitality and with what I can only describe as her *cuisine personnelle*. Fisher cooked with the seasons and used simple preparations, regularly doing all of the prep work for meals in the early hours of the morning in order to spend time with her guests when they arrived. The care and attention she brought to each occasion were evident in the smallest of details. She always toasted nuts before serving them with an aperitif of local wine or her "one-two-three" cocktail, and with her meals she usually offered wine, sourdough bread from the bakery in nearby Sonoma, and local cheese. Her table was always formally set with bread plates and cloth napkins. Above all, Fisher enjoyed her guests: she drank with them, served them, and dined with them. Sharing a meal with her, it was impossible not to remember that she had written, "There is a communion of more than our bodies when bread is broken and wine drunk." Those words echoed in the pleasure of it all.

There were many people who felt as I did that the 2008 centennial of M. F. K. Fisher's birth merited a special commemoration, and I wish to thank them for making my personal tribute, *M. F. K. Fisher among the Pots and Pans*, a reality. Darra Goldstein, founding editor of *Gastronomica* and general editor of California Studies in Food and Culture, believed in the viability of the project, and she has been a facilitator and source of encouragement during the transformation of the manuscript into a book. The University of California editorial staff, especially the lead editor, Dore Brown, have also embraced this tribute with professionalism, wisdom, and good grace. I am greatly in their debt. A thank-you must also be extended to Margo True and Sharon Silva, who copyedited the recipes and made them accessible to today's generation of cooks.

I also wish to thank M. F. K. Fisher's daughter Kennedy Friede Golden for her encouragement and gracious permission to reproduce photographs from the family's private collection. And I would like to give a special acknowledgment to Avram Dumitrescu for the evocative watercolor illustrations he contributed to the book. It was a great pleasure to work with him and with the book's designer, Sandy Drooker, who created a work of art as well as a beautiful book to honor M. F. K. Fisher's one hundredth birthday.

Amanda Hesser's tribute to M. F. K. Fisher in the fiftieth-anniversary edition of *The Art of Eating* suggested that a closer look at Fisher's role as a cook and kitchen habitué had merit. For both her insights and the foreword that she wrote to this book, I want to express my gratitude. To my agent, Doe Coover, and her assistant, Frances Kennedy, my heartfelt thanks for your edits, which always prove to be so valuable, and for doing what you do so well. And if I have unwittingly omitted anyone who contributed to this book, "I can no other answer make but thanks and thanks and ever thanks."

I

Whittier and Laguna Beach

1908–1922

Born in Albion, Michigan, on July 3, 1908, Mary Frances Kennedy was nurtured on the collective wisdom of *The Settlement Cookbook*, *The Boston Cooking-School Cookbook*, *The Miriam Cookbook*, and the "tried and true" recipes gathered and handed down to Edith Holbrook Kennedy by her mother. The transition from liquids to solids, cereals to fruit and vegetable purees, eggs to patties was well charted in those new-to-nutrition days and no doubt initiated the first stages of Mary Frances's developing palate. Of course, it is impossible to know what Edith served to her dynamic husband, Rex, when they took up housekeeping in Albion, but an extensive railroad grid had made it possible to ship foodstuffs across a country where food was becoming one of the most important industries. Libby, McNeil & Libby had built the world's largest canning factory in Sunnyvale, California; Ford had introduced a Model T that was said to be stronger than a horse and could be adapted to be an ideal pickup truck for farmers; and Ellen Swallow Richards had founded the American Economics Association to raise the status of homemaking.

In the Kennedy kitchen at 202 Irwin Avenue, Mary Frances's mother, Edith, relied on household help, as her own mother had done in Onawa,

202 Irwin Avenue, Albion, Michigan

Iowa, where Scandinavian and German girls eagerly did the cooking and other chores while learning the language of their adopted country. Edith's ideas about domestic life were undoubtedly influenced by the table set by her own mother, Mary Frances Holbrook, and by the year she had spent abroad when she was twenty-two. After Edith married Rex Kennedy, the editor of the *Albion Evening Recorder*, she served her husband meals in the dining room, a formal room with a door that separated it from the menial tasks of the kitchen. Rex liked waffles for breakfast, and Edith made them from a favorite recipe in *The Miriam Cookbook*. For dinner, she might have prepared a plump chicken from a nearby farm, or a beef roast shipped from Chicago (Albion was on the main railroad line between Chicago and Detroit). Whatever the entrée, the side dish, or the dessert, the meal would have showcased the bounty of the Midwest. And Edith would have exhibited her skill and her preference for sweets by whipping up a batch of divinity fudge or, every year on his birthday, a Lady Baltimore cake for her husband.

When Edith and Rex decided to leave Albion for the West Coast in 1911, Mary Frances was almost three and her sister, Anne, was eleven months old. The family's first stop was Spokane, where they visited Rex's youngest brother, Ted, and his parents, who had recently moved there from Iowa. Mary Frances often said that her earliest memories dated back to those months in Washington, where she saw row after row of apple trees outside of Spokane and played in abandoned rowboats on Maury Island, scooping water out of their unseaworthy bottoms. If so, did the smell of the fruit orchards and the taste of the ocean during that magical summer became a part of her food memory, and did they foreshadow her fondness for applesauce and baked apples and the compelling, briny taste of oysters? It is tempting to think so.

In *The Gastronomical Me*, Mary Frances wrote that her transformative food experiences actually began in Whittier, California, where Rex Kennedy moved his family after purchasing the local newspaper in the fall of 1912. Citrus, olive, and walnut trees grew on the outskirts of the small, predominantly Quaker community, and fields of wheat and grazing pastures stretched from Whittier west to Los Angeles. The first self-service grocery stores opened independently in various towns, and the New Nutrition advocated by Sylvester Graham and practiced by John Harvey Kellogg at the Battle Creek Sanitarium held sway, especially in the dietary requirements of Grandmother Holbrook, who had joined her daughter, son-in-law, and two granddaughters in their home at 115 Painter Avenue.

"The first thing I remember tasting and then wanting to taste again is the grayish-pink fuzz my grandmother skimmed from a spitting kettle of strawberry jam," Mary Frances wrote, describing the sight, smell, and

taste of a huge kettle of jam simmering on the stove of the kitchen on
Painter Avenue. The only room in the large, comfortable house to escape Rex's remodeling efforts, the kitchen became etched in Mary
Frances's imagination as one of the ugliest rooms she had ever known
and loved. Outfitted with a gas stove, a small icebox, and many cupboards, the room was dominated by a large table with a chipped enamel
top and bins for flour and sugar built into each side. Two small windows
high above the sink and a single bulb hanging over the table provided
the only light in the narrow room. Despite its limitations, this kitchen
became her schoolroom and playground, where from her fourth year to
her twelfth she learned the power of a delicious dish served to appreciative diners in the formal dining room on the other side of the swinging
door. There, Rex sat at one end of the table with his back to the kitchen,
and Edith positioned herself at the opposite end in order to summon the
cook of the moment by ringing a little silver bell placed without fail near
her right hand.

In *Among Friends*, a memoir of her first twelve years, Mary Frances
chronicled the "high priests and priestesses" who appeared and disap-
peared through that kitchen door during her early preschool years. A
black woman named Cynthia was the first, and Mary Frances and Anne
loved the soft hymns Cynthia hummed as she went about her work in the
kitchen. While they sat at the table in the middle of the room, Cynthia
told them stories and gave them samples of whatever she was preparing
for her evening meal. But Cynthia left after her first winter in Whittier
because she was lonely. Amimoto, an Asian student who sought to supplement his allowance by serving as houseboy, replaced her, and his
tenure was even shorter.

Later on, after all four of the McLure sisters, who lived nearby, had
taken their turn in the Kennedy kitchen, a South African woman named

Ora arrived. With her sharp knives and kitchen savvy, Ora worked transformations on everyday foods. She decorated pies with stars cut from
thinly rolled dough, shaved carrots into thin curls, and minced herbs.
During her reign, pastry fleurons and sprigs of parsley enhanced even
the lowliest dishes of hash. From Ora, Mary Frances began to learn
presentation and the subtle art of using condiments other than salt and
pepper.

Although Grandmother Holbrook and Edith usually hired the housekeeper of the moment, Rex brought other unlikely helpers into the house
on Painter Avenue. For a brief period, Mary Frances and Anne comman-
deered kitchen stools on Sunday afternoons to watch the handyman,
Charles, make butterscotch that looked like "panes of colored crystal."
Everyone rated the homemade candy second to none, until the children
innocently explained Charles's secrets to their mother. Not only did the
master candy maker forage for lollipop sticks in and around the playground at the Bailey Street School, he also protected his thumb and
forefinger with a generous amount of spittle before testing the temperature of the molten, tawny butterscotch. Shortly after these revelations,
Charles's efforts in the kitchen mysteriously ceased.

There was also a cook named Anita, whom one of Rex's friends prevailed on him to hire. She enchanted the children with stories of taking
lessons from the chef of the king of Spain, but her culinary skills were,
unfortunately, limited. To provide simple meals, Mary Frances and Anne
chopped and mashed vegetables, scrambled eggs, and made toast while
Anita spent days preparing her favorite dishes—elegant chicken enchiladas and a vanilla flan—from her limited repertoire. While Edith
Kennedy retired to her chaise longue upstairs to avoid the crashing
sounds emanating from the kitchen, Anita would turn out her flan, a perfect *crème renversée*. Mary Frances never forgot "the brown subtle liquid

running at just the proper speed over its flat surface and down its impeccably sloping sides."

Edith Kennedy, who was an avid reader, reserved her culinary activities in Whittier for the occasional dishes that she enjoyed making: egg croquettes for the family during Lent, cookies for the Christmas holidays, and an airy cheese puff for special occasions.

In daily menu planning, Edith deferred to the wishes and dietary constraints of her mother. A woman of more than a few midwestern convictions, Grandmother Holbrook clung to the habit of eating root vegetables, even though a variety of fresh vegetables was available all year long in California. She also insisted on ladling white sauce over carrots, dried beef, and virtually everything else. She would eat no fried foods or pastries, no oils, and no seasonings. Above all, she allowed no displays of "sinful" pleasure in the food served at the dining room table.

An observant child, Mary Frances realized that there was a very real connection between the food prepared in the kitchen and the ambience of the dining room. Grandmother's diet dictated menus of watery lettuce served with boiled dressing; overcooked hen accompanied by stodgy dumplings; and stewed tomatoes bound with soggy bread. Whenever Grandmother was absent, a partylike spirit prevailed. Rex served a thick broiled steak, a salad of freshly picked watercress dressed with fine olive oil, and glasses of red wine from a vineyard in nearby San Gabriel. By the time Mary Frances was six, she knew the names of several local wines and was allowed to have her own stemmed glass with a little wine that had been diluted with water. Rex also served his daughters "blotters," slices of white bread dipped into the steak's natural juices. Although these savory treats were high on their list of favorites, what they really loved was when Edith allowed them to hollow out their cupcakes and fill them with cream and sugar. They would remove the cupcake's cap, scoop out the crumbs, place

cream and sugar in the hollowed base, replace the lid, and top with more
sugar and cream. Eating this dessert slowly was a heavenly "indulgence."
The contrast between the bland, mid-Victorian meals that accommodated Grandmother's diet and Rex's favorite dishes made a lasting impression on Mary Frances, who would one day celebrate the thrill of a
freshly baked peach pie and the glory of the first peas of the season as
examples of the best meals she ever ate.

Another kitchen where memorable culinary experiences occurred was
in the home of Edith Kennedy's friend Gwendolyn Nettleship, who lived
in a shabby farmhouse on the corner of Painter and Philadelphia. Mary
Frances and Anne adored "Aunt" Gwen, a former missionary who spoke
with a British accent and read *Uncle Remus* and *The Jungle Book* to them.
The Nettleship kitchen, dominated by a large wood-burning stove and a
round table, was the congenial place where Aunt Gwen served her brothers robust meals before eating her own supper, occasionally in the company of Mary Frances and Anne. Of those shared experiences Mary
Frances wrote: "I decided at the age of nine that one of the best ways to
grow up is to eat and talk quietly with good people." Memories of the
checkered oilcloth that covered the table, the china dotted with pink
carnations, and dishes such as cocoa toast and fried egg sandwiches remained with Mary Frances throughout her life.

Soon after the Kennedys had settled in Whittier, they had acquired a
cottage forty-two miles away, in Laguna Beach. The beach house was a
retreat to which Rex and the family fled on Saturday afternoon after the
newspaper was printed. Fresh lettuces and other produce were purchased
on the Canyon Road leading into the town, and there was still enough light
to reel in a fish to fry for the evening meal. Sundays were frequently spent
in spontaneous meals with friends from Whittier, who welcomed an
invitation to relax after a week in town. Their potluck meals included

Beach house, Laguna Beach, California

homemade scones, bowls of chicken salad, and crusty bread brought from Whittier, and these dishes were often supplemented by freshly caught rock bass and Edith's prodigious batches of fried corn oysters. On Sunday afternoons, the table, which was usually centered in the sunny lean-to kitchen, was pulled into the dining room, and sometimes even lengthened so that it extended through the wide doorway into the living room, in order to accommodate all of the guests. At the beach house, Edith cooked the family's meals, and her third daughter, Norah, remembers that they were hearty and delicious. Laguna Beach offered a freer and more informal opportunity for Edith to slip out of the mode of the editor's wife who presided over a proper household.

During the summer months, when they were on vacation from school, Mary Frances and Anne stayed at the beach house with Aunt Gwen. They harvested mussels, steamed them over a makeshift coal fire outside of the kitchen, then rushed them into the house and ate them with a squeeze of lemon juice, a drizzle of melted butter, and a slice of fresh bread. Or Aunt Gwen made her special fried onions in the same pan she used to fry fish and heat breakfast, wiping the pan clean with newspaper between preparations. She sliced the onions into rings, coated them in seasoned flour, deep-fried them to a golden color, and served them with cold milk. These satisfying suppers were magical because they were delicious meals composed of only one or two dishes, consumed by hungry children who had spent a day playing on the beach.

The simplicity of the meals in Laguna Beach contrasted with the elegance of the meals in the Los Angeles restaurants where Edith occasionally took her daughters to celebrate a birthday, see a Gilbert and Sullivan performance, or attend the ballet. On her first trip to the Victor Hugo Restaurant, Mary Frances ordered chicken à la king because she had heard her mother mention the dish. This impressive outing set the standard for other special meals, which often consisted of something exotic served under glass and flambéed desserts prepared tableside. Edith and her daughters also frequented an ice cream parlor called the Pig 'n' Whistle near the Pacific Electric Depot in Los Angeles. After a day of shopping, they would sit in one of the booths and eat scoops of flavored ice cream out of long silver boats before boarding the electric train back to Whittier. Because Mary Frances and Anne were accustomed to eating at a table where children were silent unless spoken to, these dining occasions away from home made a deep impression on them. They could smile at the waiter and tell him how delicious the food tasted, and they could giggle with Edith when the ice cream melted into a colorful, rich pool. "Best of all, we talked-laughed-sang-kissed and in general exposed ourselves to sensations forbidden when the matriarchal stomach rumbled among us,"

Mary Frances wrote. "And my thoughts on how gastronomy should influence the pattern of any happy person's life became more and more firm."

It was not long before Mary Frances began to be curious about the power associated with the preparation of food and about what she could make happen when she prepared meals for the people she loved. One Sunday she volunteered to make supper for her sister and herself while her parents were visiting friends, and she chose Hindu eggs, an old standby for the cook's night off. She began by boiling eggs and slicing bread for toast. Then she consulted the *Settlement Cookbook* for a recipe to spice up the sauce and bind the dish together. She found a variation of béchamel sauce that appealed to her because the ingredients included a pinch of curry powder. Wanting to be sure that the exotic-sounding curry flavored the sauce adequately, she added more than a few teaspoons to the sauce before mixing it with the eggs and spooning the combination over pieces of toast. Anne, whether out of loyalty or fear, ate as much of the potent concoction as her older sister did. During the next few hours they drank copious amounts of milk, put soothing oil on their lips, and hoped that these remedies would bring relief to their burning mouths.

Mary Frances's next culinary effort was potentially more disastrous, as creativity once again triumphed over caution. While Edith was recovering from the birth of her third child, Norah, in the late spring of 1917, Mary Frances found a recipe in the well-worn pages of *The Invalid's Cookery Book* and prepared a bland pudding for her mother. When she unmolded it, the white pudding on its white saucer looked so unattractive that she picked a handful of black berries from a backyard bush and arranged them in a ring around the pudding. Within an hour the nurse found Edith covered with red welts and the baby screaming with hunger. The nurse summoned Rex, who in turn called the doctor, who diagnosed

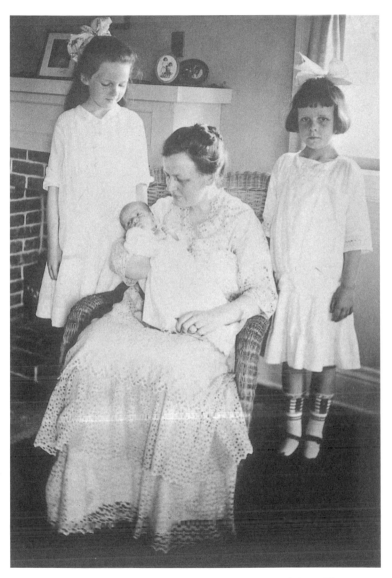

Mary Frances, Edith, Norah, and Anne, Whittier, 1917

With Norah and Aunt Gwen, Laguna Beach, 1919

food poisoning. Explanations were given, and a crushed Mary Frances retreated to the dubious comfort of *Ivanhoe*.

Although some of these failures were dramatic in their retelling, most of Mary Frances's efforts in the Painter Avenue kitchen satisfied her curiosity and were a source of pride to her mother. On Thursdays, the cook's day off, Mary Frances occasionally asked to prepare the evening meal. Having mastered white sauce by the time she was seven, she knew how to measure and sift flour and add just the right amount of butter and liquid to keep the whole thing bubbling on the stove. At the proper moment, she combined the sauce with canned tuna, chipped beef, or vegetables and served the mixture over toast. She also could poach eggs and scramble them with the appropriate heat and care. Praise for a job well done was motivation for additional experiments, and she was a quick study.

Mary Frances was able to focus on the family, and especially their meals together, because Whittier was relatively unaffected by what went on in the rest of the world. During the early years of World War I, the largely Quaker community did not experience the soaring food prices of New York, Boston, and Philadelphia, where people rioted because they could not feed their families. Although there were a few examples of anti-German sentiment, and the local butcher and sausage-maker was forced to close his shop because he was German, the pacifist community did not rally to the war effort. When America entered the war in 1917, and Rex entertained the idea of enlisting, Edith informed him that their fourth child was on the way and the family would need his presence as well as his income as co-owner and editor of the *Whittier News*.

Five months after the birth of David Holbrook Kennedy in May 1919, Rex purchased a large house and orange ranch on thirteen acres of land on a southern extension of Painter Avenue in an unincorporated area of Whittier. The Ranch, as it came to be called, brought a new freedom to

Mary Frances, Anne, Norah, and David. No longer living on a busy street in the middle of town, the Kennedy children played among the cluster of buildings that included a guesthouse, cookhouse, barn, sheds, garages, and chicken coops. They gathered flowers, climbed the fruit trees, and cared for the Ranch menagerie, which included a cow, chickens, and bees.

In contrast to their earlier kitchen, the kitchen at the Ranch was light and filled with the smells of orange blossoms, and the family meals increasingly reflected the bounty of the Ranch. And after Grandmother Holbrook died in 1921, the family's diet became positively "heathenish," according to Mary Frances. Milk, cream, and butter from the cow contributed to a rich diet of puddings and an orgy of baking. Fresh eggs were used for mayonnaise, omelets, and cakes. The orchards and citrus grove provided fruit in season, and Rex planted a vegetable garden of artichokes, asparagus, and green leafy lettuces. The meals prepared in the Ranch kitchen were adventures, and Mary Frances was an eager participant.

She learned to churn and mold butter and to assemble ingredients for cakes that Edith baked on Saturday mornings, including her annual birthday cake for Rex. In later years, Mary Frances credited her mother with teaching her the art of cake baking, especially layer cakes with various fruit and nut fillings, which she, however, rarely made. Mary Frances also prepared afternoon tea for her mother and the Whittier ladies who visited the house. Although as a teenager she complained about this responsibility, she secretly prided herself on the fact that Edith thought her tea trays second to none. This approval motivated forays into assembling nasturtium leaf sandwiches, trimmed and thinly sliced, as well as decorating dainty miniature teacakes.

Whether it was those early kitchen adventures or the simple enjoyment of sitting "before a bowl of cold white grains of rice, half-floating in the creamy milk and the brown sugar I could add from my own little pitcher or dish," or ladling warm buttery sauce over tender stalks of asparagus before arranging the vegetables over toast, or pouring "cold thick cream over the hot delights" of apple dumplings, the gift of those formative years in Whittier was an appreciation of the pleasures of the table. Mary Frances also discovered that the kitchen could be a source of personal power: "The stove, the bins, the cupboards made an inviolable throne room. From them I ruled . . . and I loved that feeling."

Fried Onion Rings

Mary Frances liked to say that onions were as much a part of her cooking as eggs and brown sugar. She added sliced sweet onions to many of her salads and braised vegetable dishes and regularly used green onions, leeks, and other members of the lily family in her cooking. Aunt Gwen's fried onion rings, probably made with bacon fat, were a particularly delicious food memory from her childhood vacation days in Laguna Beach. Re-created here, the simple dish, accompanied by only a glass of cold milk, was described by Mary Frances as a complete—and satisfying—meal. *Serves 4*

ONIONS

4 large sweet onions

1½ cups milk

1½ cups water

BATTER

1 egg

1 cup buttermilk

1 cup flour

½ teaspoon salt

½ teaspoon baking soda

Vegetable oil for deep-frying

Cut the onions into ¼-inch-thick slices, and separate the slices into rings. Combine the milk and water in a bowl, add the onion rings, and let soak for 1 hour. Remove the onion rings from the liquid and pat dry.

To make the batter: mix together the egg and buttermilk in a bowl until blended. Add the flour, salt, and baking soda and stir until smooth.

Preheat the oven to 200 degrees.

Pour oil to a depth of about 3 inches into a deep, heavy pot and heat to 375 degrees. Working in small batches, dip the onion rings into the batter and carefully slip them into the hot oil. Fry until golden brown, 2 to 3 minutes. Remove and drain on absorbent paper. Keep in the oven until all the onions are fried.

Serve piping hot.

Hindu Eggs

Adapted from An Alphabet for Gourmets

In 1949, Mary Frances "returned to the scene of the crime," revisiting a dish she had made as a young girl with little regard for the original recipe. (Quadrupling the amount of curry in the cream sauce, she served the eggs to her younger sister and ate them herself as well, to their common discomfort.) Here is a revised version that mixes curry powder into the filling and omits it in the sauce. The eggs and their sauce can be served atop toasted English muffins with a generous slice of fried Canadian or regular bacon. *Serves 6*

12 eggs, hard-boiled and peeled
¼ cup crème frâiche
¼ cup mayonnaise
1 tablespoon Dijon mustard
1 tablespoon curry powder
2 green onions, white part only, finely chopped
1 tablespoon finely chopped fresh parsley
1 tablespoon snipped fresh chives
Salt
Freshly ground white pepper

BÉCHAMEL SAUCE
2 tablespoons butter, cut into small pieces
2 tablespoons flour
½ teaspoon salt
2 cups whole milk, warmed

Pinch ground nutmeg

Ground white pepper to taste

Slice each egg in half lengthwise. Put the yolks in a bowl and mash them with the crème frâiche, mayonnaise, and mustard until smooth. Stir in the curry powder, green onions, parsley, and chives. Season to taste with salt and pepper.

Divide the yolk mixture evenly among 12 of the egg halves, mounding it slightly. Top the filled halves with the remaining halves to re-form whole eggs. Butter a shallow casserole large enough to hold the eggs in a single layer, arrange them in the casserole, cover, and refrigerate for a few hours.

Preheat the oven to 350 degrees.

To make the béchamel sauce: in a heavy saucepan, melt the butter over medium heat. Stir in the flour with a wooden spoon, add the salt, and stir constantly until smooth, 2 to 3 minutes. Gradually pour in the milk while stirring constantly, add the nutmeg and white pepper, and then continue to cook, stirring often, until the sauce coats the back of the spoon, about 10 minutes.

Cover the eggs with the warm cream sauce and place in the oven. Bake until the sauce bubbles and turns brown around the edges, 30 to 40 minutes. Serve immediately.

Edith's Cheese Puff

Adapted from *With Bold Knife and Fork*

Although she typically relied on domestics to prepare meals, Edith also had a few tricks up her sleeve for when a fast lunch or supper was needed. Known under a variety of names, this strata was one of her specialties. She passed the recipe on to her daughter, who would never have dreamed of making it with squishy-fresh bread, skim milk, or packaged cheese slices. *Serves 6*

4 eggs
2 cups whole milk
½ teaspoon salt
¼ teaspoon freshly ground white pepper
3 tablespoons butter, softened
9 slices day-old Italian bread, crusts removed
½ pound American cheddar cheese, grated

In a bowl, beat the eggs until blended. Add the milk, salt, and pepper and mix well.

Lightly butter a 2-quart soufflé dish or casserole. Spread the remaining butter on one side of the bread slices. Arrange three of the bread slices, buttered side up, in the bottom of the prepared dish, and top with half of the grated cheese. Repeat with three more bread slices and the remaining cheese. Top with the last three slices of bread. Pour the egg-milk mixture over the slices. Let stand at room temperature for at least 1 hour, or cover and refrigerate overnight.

Preheat the oven to 350 degrees. Bake until puffed and golden brown around the edges, about 1 hour. Serve immediately.

Lady Baltimore Cake

During her childhood, Mary Frances associated a Lady Baltimore cake with special occasions, like her father's birthday. Why this traditional white layer cake, which had become identified with the city of Baltimore, appealed to her mother is not known, but Edith's mother, Mary Frances Holbrook, had been employed as a governess in a southern family before she married an Iowan banker, and she likely passed the recipe on to her daughter. *Serves 10 to 12*

CAKE

3 cups cake flour, sifted
1 tablespoon baking powder
½ teaspoon salt
½ cup butter, at room temperature
1½ cups sugar
1¼ cups whole milk
1 teaspoon vanilla extract
4 egg whites, stiffly beaten

FILLING

6 dried figs
½ cup golden raisins
1 cup boiling water
1 tablespoon rum (optional)
½ cup pecan pieces, chopped

2 egg whites

1½ cups sugar

5 tablespoons water

1½ teaspoons light corn syrup

½ teaspoon vanilla extract

Preheat the oven to 375 degrees. Butter and flour two 9-inch round cake pans.

To make the cake: in a bowl, stir together the flour, baking powder, and salt. In a separate bowl, cream the butter until smooth. Add the sugar and beat, using a handheld mixer on medium speed or a wooden spoon, until light and fluffy.

Add the flour mixture to the creamed sugar and butter in 3 or 4 additions alternately with the milk in 2 or 3 additions, beginning and ending with the flour and beating after each addition until the batter is smooth. Beat in the vanilla. Gently fold the egg whites into the batter.

Divide the batter evenly between the cake pans. Bake until a tester inserted in the center of each layer comes out clean, 25 to 30 minutes. Unmold the cake layers onto wire racks and let cool completely.

Meanwhile, make the filling. In a heatproof bowl, plump the figs and raisins in the boiling water and rum, if using, until the fruits are soft, about 30 minutes. Drain and chop the fruits, return them to the bowl, and add the pecans.

To make the frosting: combine the egg whites, sugar, water, and corn syrup in a heatproof bowl, and whisk until well mixed. Place over simmering water in a saucepan. Using a whisk or a handheld mixer on high speed, beat until light and fluffy peaks form, about 7 minutes. Remove from over the water and continue to beat until cooled and thick enough to spread. Whisk in the vanilla.

Add enough of the frosting (about 1 cup) to the filling mixture to create a mixture that spreads easily. Place a cake layer on a serving plate and spread with the filling. Set the top layer in place and spread the remaining frosting on the top and sides of the cake, using small circular motions to create peaks.

Nasturtium-Leaf Sandwiches

The nasturtium plant, also known as Indian cress or Peruvian cress because it originated in South America, is prized for its bright-colored, trumpet-shaped blossoms, plump seedpods, and circular leaves—all of them edible. The leaves' peppery flavor, reminiscent of watercress, increases with the temperature of the growing area, but other foods quickly tame it. Little wonder, then, that Mary Frances, who loved watercress as a child, tucked nasturtium leaves into the dainty sandwiches she served at her mother's teas. *Makes about 40*

1 loaf white Pullman bread, crust removed, sliced lengthwise into
    three 1-inch slices
3/4 cup butter, softened
2 cups nasturtium leaves, lightly packed
Nasturtium blossoms for garnish

Using a rolling pin, firmly roll each slice of bread to flatten. Spread each slice on one side with butter.

Reserve 6 nasturtium leaves for garnish. Finely chop the rest of the leaves. Spread the chopped leaves over the buttered side of each bread slice. Then, starting from a long side, roll up each slice into a log. Wrap each log separately in plastic wrap and refrigerate until the butter has hardened, about 2 hours. (Once the butter is hard, the logs will stay rolled.)

Cut the chilled logs crosswise into 3/4-inch-thick slices. Arrange the slices on a platter and serve garnished with nasturtium blossoms and the reserved leaves.

II

At Boarding School

1923–1928

Attending schools away from Whittier provided more important opportunities for Mary Frances to develop an unprejudiced palate and an appreciation of the complexities involved in assuaging human hunger. As a boarder for a year at the Bishop's School in La Jolla, she found the dining room to be a continual source of wonderment. There, a corps of young Filipino waiters served the giggly girls, offering them savory soups and presenting dishes ornamented with carved radishes, sculpted carrots, and intricately cut celery sticks. What Mary Frances and her fellow students devoured in the private school, whose purpose she always said was to educate the future wives of Episcopalian ministers, she pronounced "the best institutional food in America."

The students spooned local Torrey pine honey over the hot biscuits they ate for breakfast, and they spread chive butter over the crispy fish served on Fridays. During the annual Old Girls' Day, the younger students feasted on fried chicken and deviled eggs, which were brought in huge baskets to the beach by the house boys. At the annual Christmas party, Mary Frances swallowed raw oysters served on the half shell and never forgot the briny, chilled sensation of the ocean in her mouth. There were also trips to the soda fountains in La Jolla, made with the permission of the house mother, and visits to the local tearoom in the company of one of the instructors.

At the Bishop's School, she also delighted in secret indulgences. Because the students were allowed to purchase one chocolate bar every day, Mary Frances was able to accumulate six or seven during the week. Then, on Saturday, she would leisurely and deliberately eat all of the bars in the solitude of her room, sometimes alternating a bite of chocolate with a bite of a salty cracker and at other times unwrapping them one by one and slowly eating the pieces while reclining on a heap of pillows, sultan-style. These indulgences became the subject of many of her stories, and they perhaps hint at an explanation for many of her favorite foods, an occasional preference for solitary dining, and her desire for privacy in the kitchen.

Mary Frances also experienced other palate-pleasers during her semesters away from home. After the Bishop's School, both Mary Frances and Anne transferred to Miss Harker's School, near Stanford University in Palo Alto. The city of San Francisco was only a bus ride away, and the Kennedy sisters frequently spent Saturday afternoons roaming Chinatown and visiting the outdoor markets where vendors sold hot pork buns and other Asian specialties. Fisherman's Wharf, with its purveyors of freshly cracked crab, and Gump's luxury store became frequent destinations as well. Occasionally they were escorted to the Palm Court or other fine San Francisco dining rooms by their Uncle Evans, who was a visiting professor at Stanford. And whenever Edith visited, she took her daughters to many of her favorite restaurants in the city that had been her escape hatch since she and Rex discovered San Francisco's cosmopolitan charm in 1915, when they visited the Pacific Panama Exhibition. Edith, Mary Frances, and Anne ate Melba toast sliced thin as tissue paper at the Garden Court and bought Ghirardelli chocolate in the shops in Union Square.

Although Mary Frances frequently downplayed her academic achievements, she took courses in Spanish, Latin, history, general science, and the Bible and consistently earned high grades, but it was in her English classes that she excelled. She wrote poems and stories for the school yearbook at both the Bishop's School and Miss Harker's, and she secretly took pride in her early work, even requesting that one of her high school stories be included in what would become the first of her posthumous books, *To Begin Again.*

After graduation from high school, Mary Frances spent the summer of 1927 at the Laguna Beach house, toying with the idea of college but not taking serious steps to select and enroll in a school. Her parents, disturbed by their daughter's lack of interest in continuing her education, urged her to join her cousin Nan at Illinois College in Jacksonville, Illinois. The prospect had an immediate appeal for Mary Frances, who loved the idea of leaving home, buying a new wardrobe for the colder weather of the Midwest, and going to a coed college. Uncle Evans accompanied her on the train as far as Chicago, introducing her to the stops along the way that featured Fred Harvey restaurants and insisting that she broaden her palate by ordering dishes in the dining car that were new to her, such as avocado cocktails, grilled sweetbreads, and wild asparagus, rather than the familiar lamb chops and banal mushrooms.

The novelty of being away from California soon waned when she discovered that the food served in the college dining hall was almost inedible. In protest against what they described as an everyday menu of cabbage, parsnips, and turnips, Mary Frances, Nan, and Nan's roommate made frequent trips to the Waffle and Coffee Shop in town. They began to eat their meals in their dormitory rooms, where they consumed ginger ale, hard rolls, cream cheese, anchovy paste, bottled French dressing, and heads of fresh lettuce. On Sundays, they got up early to indulge in hot cinnamon buns, the only acceptable fare available in the cafeteria. But these meager compensations did not cancel out either the monotony of the dining hall menu or Mary Frances's lack of enthusiasm for classes. She happily returned to California at the end of the first semester.

While the semester away at college had not enhanced her academic record, the discovery that almost everyone has something she secretly longs to eat, that almost everyone has a hunger so strong it must be satisfied, had been reinforced when she seized on every package of oranges that Edith sent and spent most of her allowance on expensive heads of fresh lettuce. And she decided that her practice of indulging in secret foods in high school had not been a passing teenage preoccupation but was a vital part of her life, one that had been nurtured in the bounty of California's soil, encouraged by the seasonal foodstuffs that she had known since childhood, and defined by certain foods that provided gratification.

Returning to Whittier, Mary Frances followed a pattern that had been established during her prep school years and transferred from one college to another, unable to find a school or course of study that captured her interest for more than a semester or two. She dreamed of action, of escaping from the stifling atmosphere of small-town California. And then her dream was realized. During a summer session at UCLA she met an attractive Princeton graduate, Alfred Young Fisher. Tall, handsome, and six years her senior, Al was the son of an Episcopalian minister. He was also under contract to teach at the Princeton Preparatory School in Cody, Wyoming, that fall. His attraction to Mary Frances's soft voice and striking beauty was immediate, and Mary Frances secretly thought that

Anne Kennedy, who enrolled with Mary Frances
at Occidental College in fall 1928

On her wedding day, September 5, 1929. Photo by George Hurrell.

Al's youthful good looks and desire to write poetry made him a modern-day Shelley. They promised to write to each other.

What started as a more or less casual correspondence became a serious epistolary courtship when Al sent love sonnets to her and shared his plans to pursue a doctoral degree in English literature in France the following year. Mary Frances and Anne had enrolled at Occidental College for the fall, but although Mary Frances went out with a few of the campus heroes, she soon let it be known that she was not really "interested in dating because she had an off-campus romance well into gear," and she was just marking time there. With very little urging, she agreed to become Mrs. Alfred Fisher when Al returned to Los Angeles at the end of the school term.

Mary Frances and Al were married on September 5, 1929. Eleven days later, traveling in student third class, they crossed the Atlantic on the *Berengaria*, spending most of the voyage getting to know each other more intimately than their year-long correspondence had allowed. The other passengers assigned to their less-than-glamorous third-class dining room seemed as uninteresting as the food, and they often skipped the ship's meals, preferring to nibble from the baskets of grapes and other fresh fruits that had been sent to their quarters by relatives, as the newlyweds anticipated their arrival in France.

Oyster Loaf

Adapted from *Consider the Oyster*

Oh, for the boarding schools of yesteryear, where teenage girls like Mary Frances feasted on oysters on the half shell, and where her mother before her reveled in oyster loaves and ginger beer during secret midnight suppers. "I know I shall never taste one [oyster loaf] like it, except in my dreams, nor will my mother . . . if she ever really did so," Mary Frances wrote. "But I can see it, and smell it, and I even know which parts to bite and which to let melt against the roof of my mouth, exquisitely hot and comforting." Here, then, is Mary Frances's version of "such schoolgirl *gourmandise.*" Serve with tartar sauce if desired. *Serves 4 to 6*

24 shucked medium oysters
1/2 cup flour
1/2 teaspoon paprika
1 teaspoon salt
Freshly ground black pepper
1 egg
1 tablespoon water
1/2 cup fine dried bread crumbs
One 10-inch round loaf French bread
1/2 cup melted butter
Vegetable oil for deep-frying

Preheat the oven to 400 degrees.

Pat the oysters dry. In a shallow bowl, mix the flour with the paprika, salt, and a few grinds of pepper. In another bowl, combine the egg and the water. Place the bread crumbs in a third bowl. Dip the oysters into the flour mixture, then into the egg mixture, and then into the crumbs. Place the oysters on a baking sheet and refrigerate for 15 minutes.

Slice the top from the bread and scoop out the insides, leaving a generous shell. Brush the cavity and the inside of the lid with the melted butter and place on a baking sheet. Bake until golden brown, about 15 minutes. Keep warm.

Pour oil to a depth of about 3 inches into a deep, heavy pot and heat to 375 degrees. Fry the oysters in batches until golden brown and crisp, 2 to 3 minutes. Remove and drain on absorbent paper. Keep warm.

Fill the cavity with the oysters, replace the lid, cut into wedges, and serve.

III

From Dijon to Eagle Rock

1929–1936

Married, almost twenty-one, and an émigrée from a small California town, Mary Frances, now Madame Fisher, came of age in France, where she discovered the differences between the ever-changing American palate and the French palate, which had been cultivated by tradition and the glories of Burgundy's wine. Her first introduction to French food occurred on the boat train from Cherbourg to Paris, and Mary Frances often spoke of it as her "most memorable meal." A porter served crusty bread, a salad of just-picked tiny lettuces, Petits Suisses cheese, robust apples, country red wine, and strong bitter coffee. "I picked up a last delicious crust-crumb from the table, smiled dazedly at my love, peered incredulously at a great cathedral on the horizon, and recognized myself as a new-born sentient human being, ready at last to *live*."

When the newlyweds arrived in Dijon, they stayed in a hotel for the first few weeks, because Al had expected to spend only a month in Dijon in an intensive language course before proceeding to Strasbourg to work toward his doctoral degree. But under the influence of a congenial professor at the University of Dijon, Al decided to remain in the Burgundian city for his graduate work. Mary Frances soon found a pension for them to live in on the rue du Petit-Potet, a short distance from the rue Chabot-Charny. She then enrolled in language classes at the university, took evening courses in sculpture at the Beaux-Arts, and earned a small amount of money tutoring students in English.

After they were settled in their two far-from-luxurious rooms—which did, however, have electricity and a gas hot plate for heating cold water— the Fishers celebrated their one-month wedding anniversary with a dinner *de luxe au prix fixe* at Ribaudot's Aux Trois Faisans, one of Dijon's oldest and most-respected restaurants. The restaurant became Mary Frances's favorite place. Although the carpets were spotted and the dining room was dingy, in a short time she discovered the glories of the sauces that the French chef prepared in the kitchen. She wrote to her sister Norah, saying that she hoped that she, too, would one day have the experience of tasting French cuisine in France, where it was taken seriously and had an ardent following in all ranks of society.

Mary Frances quickly learned about the shopping patterns of her landlady, Madame Ollagnier, who patronized specialty shops, where the green grocer offered fruits and vegetables, the butcher provided oxtails and leg of lamb, the *boulanger* baked fresh croissants, brioche, and baguettes, the *fromager* offered a selection of cheeses, the wine merchant featured local wines, and the *pâtissier* artfully supplied the desired tart. This type of shopping was not what Mary Frances had experienced in American grocery stores or self-service markets that catered to a nation on the move. France, she discovered, was not a country where people combined other activities with eating.

The daily meals prepared in the pension by Madame Ollagnier were magical transformations of cast-off bananas, sprouting potatoes, and soured cream, which Madame got for almost nothing from the neighborhood storekeepers, who cringed when she approached their shops with her black string bag. After shopping, she continued her tyranny in the windowless cubbyhole of the family kitchen, which was not more than nine feet square. She rattled the pots and pans and shouted at the servant to stretch the ingredients, water down the wine, and not waste even a crust of stale bread. Miraculously, the meals she served to her boarders were always delicious, and while she dashed between the kitchen and dining room, Monsieur Ollagnier shared with the Fishers his admiration for his hometown hero, Brillat-Savarin, as well as some of his aged pâtés. Mary Frances always said that Madame Ollagnier had "a kind of avaricious genius that could have made boiled shoe taste like milk-fed lamb *à la mode printanière*," and she always had an affection for her first landlady.

Seven months later, when the Rigoulot family acquired the pension on the rue du Petit-Potet from the Ollagniers, they also inherited the young American couple who occupied the two rooms at the back and top of the house. Mary Frances and Al were the first boarders that Madame Rigoulot had ever fed at her table, and the extravagant midday meals she prepared for them and for her family far surpassed the nourishing ragouts thriftily concocted under Madame Ollagnier's scrutinizing eye. Madame Rigoulot's father, a famous *confiseur-pâtissier* from Alsace, made apple tarts for Sunday dinner. And the family as well as the boarders enjoyed *diplomate au kirsch*, champagne and truffled geese, soufflés, salads, and chilled fruits in wine and cream on birthdays and saints' days. They were some of the headiest dishes Mary Frances had ever tasted.

Years later, Mary Frances was sorry she had refused cooking lessons when Madame Rigoulot offered them to her, but by a kind of osmosis she somehow learned about omelets, salads, roasted meats, and sauces both natural and concocted. She listened while Madame's father taught the three Rigoulot children the history of carp dumplings and sauce Soubise, and she observed with high interest the elaborate process of preparing *escargots d'or*. She also watched the chronically unhappy Madame Rigoulot assuage her misery with rich soups, tarts, and *truffes en chocolat*. Mary Frances would later comment that "this poor wracked harried creature never faltered in the way she nourished [them]. No matter what her monetary anguish, she never used false butter, nor bruised peaches, nor cut wine."

While living in Dijon, Mary Frances and Al sampled the wines of France at the annual Foire Gastronomique and tasted the traditional dishes of Burgundy in their favorite restaurants. They celebrated special occasions at Aux Trois Faisans, ate tournedos Rossini at the Buffet de la Gare, and ventured to nearby Beaune and to distant Marseille and Cassis. The steady flow of wines, eaux-de-vie, and brandies, and the abundance of fruits, vegetables, and farm-raised meats and poultry defined France as an overwhelmingly rural nation, where people from urban areas as well as farms enjoyed the bounty of the seasons. Strawberries in spring were followed by raspberries, cherries, and melons in summer, by plums and pears in autumn, and then by apples in winter. Living as they did in a city surrounded by vineyards, the Fishers learned that there was a time to prune, a time to cultivate, and then a time to harvest. For Mary Frances, "fresh and seasonal" became a way of life.

In France, she also learned the value the French placed on skill; they called it *métier*, "knowledgeability in one's role." Whether one was a waiter, an *écailler* (opener of oysters), or a writer, professionalism and a sense of excellence were expected, and Mary Frances slowly adopted a style in both her life and her writing that seemed effortless and often belied the seriousness of her purpose and skill.

Several developments influenced the Fishers' decision to leave the pension on the rue du Petit-Potet in 1931. Mary Frances had been taking art and language classes at a local university, but she had not distinguished herself academically, and she decided that she would have to prove herself another way. For the past two years she had also been writing unpublishable stories modeled on popular women's magazine fiction. Now she began thinking about writing accounts of her wanderings through the narrow Dijon streets and through the vineyards of the surrounding countryside. The pension was cramped, however, and she needed a more congenial place to write. Her younger sister Norah had also come to Dijon to study French, and Mary Frances wanted a larger apartment where Norah could visit when she had free time.

So while Al was preparing to defend his doctoral dissertation, Mary Frances took the first step in developing her own *cuisine personnelle* when she found a small apartment in the working quarter of the city on the rue Monge, two floors above a cake shop called Au Fin Gourmet. The apartment consisted of a room with an alcove for the bed, a cupboard called *la chambre noire*, and a tiny kitchen. There was a faucet on the landing outside the door that supplied water for washing and cooking. With two large windows, the main room was light and airy, and after they moved their trunks and books into the room, it became homey and hospitable.

Mary Frances's first kitchen measured just five feet long by three feet wide. In order to cook on the two-burner gas hot plate that sat on a small, rickety table, Mary Frances had to prop open the door to the main room, and when she baked, she had to place a little tin oven on top of the hot plate. Two weak shelves, which slanted slightly toward an uneven floor

First kitchen on rue Monge, Dijon, France

of baked tiles that had been scoured to a mellow pink, provided the only storage space for cooking utensils and supplies. Despite its small size, the kitchen was workable. At one end, a floor-to-ceiling window flooded the room with light. When the window was open, Mary Frances could see the tops of the trees in the square below, and she could hear the splash of a fountain as well as the footsteps of the many people visiting the outdoor market, Les Halles, which provided fruits, vegetables, meats, cheeses, and eggs to the neighborhood.

To keep butter fresh and salad greens crisp without ice posed a daily challenge, but it was in the miniscule kitchen on the rue Monge that Mary Frances began real day-to-day cooking. She soon acquired three or four pots and pans, serving pieces, glassware, and a clay casserole. She joined the housewives who shopped at the market on Wednesdays and Saturdays, and she quickly discovered which vendor had the best beefsteak and which offered the finest cheeses. She also visited the local shops, where she befriended merchants who willingly shared their cooking secrets when she purchased a head of cauliflower or a kilo of green beans.

Parting company with the rich and elaborate cuisine of Madame Rigoulot's dining room, Mary Frances devised satisfying menus of three simple courses to share with the friends who wove their way through the crowded streets of the working-class quarter to the Fishers' home. When Norah had a free Thursday afternoon, she took a bus from school to the apartment, where Mary Frances gave her fresh milk, honey, sweet butter, and the Dijon gingerbread called *pavé de santé*. She often served a simple vegetable casserole to Al's fellow graduate students. "There in Dijon, the cauliflowers were small and very succulent," she wrote, and the Gruyère cheese was grated in the market "while you watched, in a soft cloudy pile, onto your piece of paper." She also managed to grill a steak on top of the hot plate and to bake fish and fresh mushrooms in the makeshift oven. The entrée was always accompanied by bread, wine, and a salad of fresh greens or marinated beans, peppers, and endive. She purchased ripe cheese, fruit, or, on special occasions, tarts from one of the best pâtisseries for dessert.

The sheer difficulty of marketing, preserving foodstuffs, and preparing meals in a kitchen that offered so little convenience required Mary Frances to simplify the meals she served. But conviction also contributed to her emerging culinary style. She cooked meals that she hoped would "shake [her guests] from their routines, not only of meat-potatoes-gravy, but of thought, of behavior." Gaining confidence in her growing culinary expertise, she became more convinced than ever that she had a right to indulge her gastronomic prejudices in her own kitchen, and her belief that "a complete lack of caution is perhaps one of the true signs of a real gourmet" evolved in that first kitchen on the rue Monge.

What also evolved was Mary Frances's definition of an "ideal kitchen." Cleanliness was a must. Enough space to prepare a good meal for six people was another requisite, along with light and air from one or more windows. Her most important need was to be alone. Beyond these requirements, an ideal kitchen could be enhanced by a kitchen garden, a patio for summer suppers, and a view of the sea or the scent of an apple orchard. "Instead of curtains," she wrote, "I would have Venetian blinds, of four different colors for the four seasons of the year. . . . And the stove would be black, with copper and earthenware utensils to put on it. . . . There are other things, too, that would be very pleasant, like a little side-kitchen in which to make the ices and salads and tarts that should not be near the heat and high flavour of roasting meats . . . and a radio or an automatic phonograph to make dull tasks agreeable."

When Al completed his doctoral degree in the late fall of 1931, the Fishers decided to journey to Strasbourg for the holidays and a few months of research for Al. Heady with the success of her first apartment on the rue Monge, Mary Frances wanted to continue housekeeping. So, she and Al rented an apartment across from the local zoo, but it proved to be un-heatable, dismal, and depressing. A single wood-burning stove in the main room provided heat for all three rooms. Mary Frances had to cook with a coat on to keep warm, and icicles formed on the kitchen's tin roof from the steam of the boiling water. Without a friendly Les Halles just minutes away, she had to take two trams to the markets, a journey of three miles. With Mary Frances in tears almost daily, Al hastily moved them into a warm, clean pension.

Then in March, Mary Frances, Al, and Norah journeyed south to to spend their remaining few months in Cros-de-Cagnes, a small village between Nice and Antibes. They ate most of their meals at their pension and in the local café. But Al had also made the acquaintance of César, the larger-than-life village butcher, and he was invited to the bacchanalian meals of simmering stews, stacks of lusty steaks, and kegs of red wine that the butcher offered to the men of the fishing village but not to their wives. Sensual in his pursuit of lusty women as well as lusty food, César truly believed rare beef and red wine were essential to masculine desire, and he shared his bounty. For the first time, Mary Frances realized that there were not only personal "secret indulgences" but also deep hungers re-lated to a mysterious gender divide that some individuals needed to sat-isfy. And from this time forward she began to think about food in a more dimensional way, noting, especially, the food preferences of her family and friends and questioning the influences of childhood on their food choices.

When the Fishers returned to the States in the summer of 1932, the economic stresses of the Depression and the scarcity of white-collar jobs forced them to take up residence in the Kennedy beach house in Laguna

With Al Fisher, Laguna Beach, 1932

Beach. There, in her mother's kitchen, Mary Frances tried to recapture the simple meals of her childhood as well as prepare the little casseroles and gratins she had served on the rue Monge, but she soon discovered that her culinary priorities were not in sync with America's. At the Chicago World's Fair in 1933, vitamin-fortified milk, margarine, chocolate chip cookies, Miracle Whip salad dressing, and canned pineapple juice shared the spotlight with paraffin-lined milk cartons, electric Frigidaires, and improved gas stoves. Although these developments were touted as domestic progress, the cream available in America was thin in comparison to the unpasteurized thick cream at Les Halles; the cheese was tasteless, and the vegetables sadly lacking in flavor.

Furthermore, the early 1930s was a time of change both in Laguna Beach and in the lives of the people who sought refuge there. Developers wanted to widen roads, improve beaches, and build vacation homes. Resident artists, like Dillwyn Parrish and his actress wife, Gigi, who rented the house next door to the Fishers and spent their weekends there, were antipathetic to the hullabaloo of growth, preferring to retreat into their shabby studios to paint, write, and sculpt. Seeking a timely subject, Mary Frances wrote an article about the changing village, illustrated it with three drawings, and sent it to *Westways*, a travel magazine. It was the first article she published and received payment for, and seeing her words in print convinced her that writing was something she wanted to do, whether it had value to anyone else or not.

Meanwhile, in the fall of 1934, Al acquired a position as an English instructor at Occidental College, and the Fishers moved to Eagle Rock, near Pasadena. With the help of Dillwyn and Gigi, they painted and fixed up an old house, and they continued to socialize with their former neighbors in Eagle Rock and at the Parrishes' home in Laurel Canyon. Al seemed in his element teaching freshman courses, and Mary Frances found a part-time job in a greeting card shop. She spent her mornings in the Los Angeles Public Library reading old cookery books.

Perhaps it was boredom or perhaps it was a desire to dazzle and amuse another person that motivated Mary Frances to begin writing short, witty, gastronomic pieces. Whatever her motivation, reading her essays aloud soon became a pleasing prelude to dinner whenever the Parrishes visited. Before long, Mary Frances found an appreciative audience and, to Al's chagrin, a mentor in Dillwyn. At his urging, she eventually assembled her short pieces about Roman, medieval, Elizabethan, and Victorian foodways into a folder and gave him a copy, which he passed along to his sister, an established novelist. Anne Parrish in turn forwarded the manuscript, called *Serve It Forth*, to her editor at Harper's, who showed great interest in it.

Embedded within the collection of jaunty tales about Greek honey and garum, Apicius's recipes and Carême's *pièces montées*, Lucullan feasts and monastic fasts, Mary Frances developed essays that reflected the subtleties of her various food experiences: ordering a German pancake with applesauce at Henry's on Hollywood Boulevard, secretly indulging in toasted tangerine segments in a pension in Strasbourg, smelling and tasting *pain d'épice* in Dijon, and partnering chocolate with fresh bread on an outing in the Côte d'Or. In her introduction, Mary Frances said that she was writing "about eating and about what to eat and about people who eat." The book turned out to be the first of her many explorations into food memory.

When Dillwyn and Gigi separated in 1935, Dillwyn unhappily withdrew to his family's estate in Delaware. In early 1936, he and his mother invited Mary Frances to go to Europe with them for two months as a translator and guide, and Al voiced no objection. The trip provided Mary Frances with an opportunity to reexamine her relationship with Al and her long-suppressed feelings for Dillwyn, which, it seems, had been mutual. During the February crossing aboard the *Hansa*, she and Dillwyn became lovers. Their days began at noon with a glass of beer in the bar before they joined Mrs. Parrish in the dining room for galantine of veal, steak au poivre, choucroute garnie, or the Mexican, Italian, or Swedish luncheon du jour. They ended their leisurely day at midnight, again sitting in the bar, talking, drinking champagne, and eating thin rare beef sandwiches.

The unlikely trio visited the European cities where Dillwyn's mother had studied painting years earlier, including cities in the south of France, Switzerland, and England. When they were in Dijon, Mary Frances eagerly returned to Ribaudot's Aux Trois Faisans with Dillwyn to introduce him to the food and service that for her epitomized French cuisine. Dining at the familiar restaurant and looking across the ancient tiled roofs of Dijon, she contemplated the subtle and enduring meaning of those historic reminders of the past. Dillwyn proposed a fitting toast: "I drink to our pasts—to yours and mine. And to ours. The wine is strong. Time is strong too." Soon after, Mary Frances wrote an account of their visit to Ribaudot's restaurant titled "The Standing and the Waiting," and it became the centerpiece of *Serve It Forth*. Before Mrs. Parrish, Dillwyn, and Mary Frances left Europe, she met with editors at Harper's offices in London and they told her that they wanted to publish *Serve It Forth* as a "Harper Find" in both America and Britain. Mary Frances knew that she had found her future.

In May, Mary Frances returned to America more in love with Dillwyn than she thought possible, although neither knew what to do next. Respecting the status quo, Dillwyn accompanied his mother back to Delaware and Mary Frances boarded a train bound for California, where she found Al greatly changed. No longer satisfied with the gratins and casseroles they had been accustomed to eating, he began to insist on the foods his mother had served to her family, foods he believed were associated with "marital happiness"—roast beef, mashed potatoes, and chocolate cake for Sunday dinner. Mary Frances, on the other had, had just spent two months traveling and dining on the Continent, and she was not about to adopt the role of a minister's son's wife or even a faculty wife, which she suspected was Al's intent and another sign of their incompatibility.

The unexpected happened when Dillwyn invited the Fishers to join him in Switzerland to establish an artists' colony at Le Paquis, a two-storied vigneron's stone cottage he and his sister had purchased in the foothills above the town of Vevey. Without considering the consequences to his career or his marriage, Al persuaded Mary Frances to accept the offer, and the Fishers left California for Europe in the fall of 1936.

Lamb à la Mode Printanière

Despite its French name, this is a simple lamb stew with spring vegetables, and Mary Frances's remembrance of it goes back to her early initiation into *la cuisine de la mère* in the pension on the rue du Petit-Potet in Dijon. She later wrote that she concocted her stews by a subtle kind of osmosis and rarely cooked the same stew twice, but this celebration of spring, which she described as "edible and consistently interesting," was an exception. *Serves 6*

1¾ pounds boneless lamb shoulder, cut into 1½-inch chunks
Salt
Freshly ground black pepper
1 tablespoon olive oil, or as needed
1 cup sliced onions
1 tablespoon flour
1 teaspoon sugar
1¼ cups beef stock
½ cup dry red wine
1 cup peeled and chopped tomatoes
1 sprig rosemary
1 clove garlic, minced
6 baby turnips, trimmed and peeled
6 small carrots, trimmed and peeled
12 pearl onions, blanched in boiling water and peeled
1 cup shelled peas
6 small potatoes, peeled (optional)

Season the meat with salt and pepper. In a Dutch oven or other deep, heavy pot, heat the 1 tablespoon oil over medium heat. Add the onions and sauté until tender, about 5 minutes. Remove to a bowl. Add more oil to the pot, if necessary, and, working in batches to avoid crowding, brown the meat on all sides over medium-high heat.

Return all of the meat to the pot, sprinkle with the flour and sugar, and cook, stirring, until the flour is absorbed. Return the sautéed onions to the pot and add the stock, wine, tomatoes, rosemary, and garlic. Bring to a boil, reduce the heat to low, cover, and simmer until the lamb is tender, about 1½ hours.

Meanwhile, bring a saucepan filled with water to a boil, add the turnips, and simmer until just tender, about 10 minutes. Drain and set aside. Separately cook the carrots, onions, peas, and potatoes, if using, in the same way, adjusting the timing as necessary.

About 15 minutes before the lamb is tender, remove and discard the rosemary sprig and add all of the cooked vegetables to the pot. When the stew is ready, taste and correct the seasoning. Serve hot.

Madame Rigoulot's Cheese Soufflé
Adapted from *With Bold Knife and Fork*

The flour, cheese, and eggs that Mary Frances's Dijon landlady used more than seventy-five years ago are unlike today's pasteurized and enriched ingredients. Her method of making a soufflé may also raise an eyebrow or two, but Mary Frances preserved it in memory of the best domestic cook she ever met. *Serves 4*

¾ cup grated Gruyère cheese
1 cup whole milk
3 tablespoons flour
6 eggs
4 tablespoons butter, melted
Salt
Freshly ground white pepper

Preheat the oven to 400 degrees. Butter a 6-cup soufflé dish and dust with ¼ cup of the grated cheese.

In a saucepan, stir together the milk and flour until smooth.

Separate the eggs, placing the yolks in one bowl and the whites in another. Add half of the egg yolks and all of the butter to the milk mixture and stir to combine. Place the saucepan over low heat and cook, stirring, until the mixture begins to thicken, about 10 minutes. Add the rest of the egg yolks to the pan while stirring constantly. Then gradually add the remaining ½ cup cheese, stirring until melted. Season to taste with salt and pepper. Remove from the heat.

Using a whisk or a handheld mixer on medium-high speed, beat the egg whites until stiff. Gently fold the egg whites into the egg-cheese soufflé base just until combined.

Transfer to the soufflé dish and place in the oven. Immediately reduce the heat to 375 degrees and bake until the soufflé rises about 2 inches above the dish rim and is golden brown on top, 25 to 30 minutes. Serve immediately.

Cauliflower Casserole

This simple casserole of cauliflower in Mornay sauce was a staple of Mary Frances's kitchen on the rue Monge. If dining alone with Al, she served it as a first course. If she was entertaining, it became a tasty side dish to accompany a steak or a chop. *Serves 4*

Salt

1 head cauliflower, separated into florets

½ cup grated Gruyère cheese, or ¼ cup each grated Gruyère
    and Parmesan cheese

1 cup béchamel sauce (½ recipe from Hindu Eggs, page 26), warm

Freshly ground black pepper

Pinch of ground nutmeg or cayenne pepper

¼ cup fresh bread crumbs

2 tablespoons butter, melted

Preheat the oven to 375 degrees. Butter a 9-inch baking dish.

Bring a saucepan filled with water to a boil. Add 1½ to 2 tablespoons salt and blanch the cauliflower florets until a knife pierces the stem of a floret easily, about 10 minutes. Drain, refresh under cold running water, and drain again.

Add the cheese to the warm béchamel sauce, converting it to a Mornay sauce. Stir until smooth. Spoon about one-third of the warm sauce over the bottom of the baking dish. Arrange the cauliflower on top and season with salt, black pepper, and nutmeg. Pour the rest of the sauce over the top, sprinkle with the bread crumbs, and drizzle with the butter.

Bake until the bread crumbs are browned and the sauce is bubbly, about 20 minutes. Serve hot.

Galantine of Veal

Adapted from *House Beautiful*

To celebrate the coming of spring, Mary Frances recommended a menu featuring asparagus, fresh herbs, and young veal. Long a favorite in the French culinary repertoire, and especially in French restaurants and on ocean liners' buffet tables, the dish might be served cold in its golden jelly as a galantine. If it is served hot, sometimes referred to as a ballotine, a puree of spinach and sorrel and a fine Bordeaux wine would be good companions. *Serves 6*

One 6-pound shoulder of veal

STOCK

2 carrots, chopped

2 onions, chopped

2 stalks celery, trimmed and chopped

4 lecks, white part only, chopped

1 cup dry white wine

Bouquet garni of parsley, thyme, and bay leaf

10 cups cold water

Salt

Freshly ground black pepper

STUFFING

½ pound calves' liver, cut into chunks

½ pound ham, cut into chunks

1 cup fresh bread crumbs

¼ cup snipped fresh chives

¼ cup minced fresh parsley
1 tablespoon chopped fresh basil
1 tablespoon chopped fresh thyme
4 tablespoons butter
1 large clove garlic, finely chopped
1 white onion, chopped
½ cup salted pistachio nuts
1 whole egg, plus 1 egg yolk, lightly beaten
Salt
Freshly ground black pepper

2 cups dry white wine
2 carrots, peeled and coarsely chopped
2 stalks celery, trimmed and coarsely chopped
1 bay leaf

Ask your butcher to bone and butterfly the veal shoulder, reserving the bones and scraps, or bone it yourself. Refrigerate the shoulder until ready to stuff.

To make the stock: in a large pot, combine the veal bones and scraps, carrots, onions, celery, leeks, wine, bouquet garni, and water. Bring almost to a boil over medium-high heat, skimming off any foam. Reduce the heat to low and simmer uncovered, skimming as needed, for about 3 hours. Strain through a fine-mesh sieve into a clean saucepan, and then boil down until reduced to 6 cups. Remove from the heat, season to taste with salt and pepper, and set aside.

To make the stuffing: grind the liver and ham in a meat grinder, saving the juices.

In a large bowl, combine the liver, ham, bread crumbs, chives, parsley, basil, and thyme. In a skillet, melt the butter over medium heat, add the garlic and onion, and sauté lightly until tender, about 10 minutes. Add to the liver mixture along with the nuts and mix well. Mix in the egg and egg yolk and season with salt and pepper. Lay the boned veal shoulder, cut side up, on a work surface, and spread the stuffing evenly over the surface. Roll the veal up tightly, wrap in cheesecloth, and tie securely with kitchen string.

Pour the reduced veal stock and the wine into a large pot and add the carrots, celery, and bay leaf. Bring to a boil, add the rolled veal, reduce the heat to low, cover, and simmer, turning every hour, for 4 hours. Remove from the heat.

To serve the veal cold, as a galantine, let cool completely in the broth. Transfer the veal to a platter, reserving the broth, and refrigerate until well chilled. Strain the broth through a fine-mesh sieve lined with cheesecloth and chill until slightly thickened. Snip the string and carefully unwrap the veal, keeping it seam side down on the platter. Coat the chilled galantine with some of the broth, cover with plastic wrap, and return to the refrigerator. Pour the remaining broth into a shallow pan and chill until it thickens and sets.

Cut the galantine crosswise into 1½-inch-thick slices, and arrange the slices on a serving plate. Cut the jellied broth into cubes, arrange around the slices, and serve.

To serve the veal hot, as a ballotine, remove it from the hot broth and place on a platter. Strain the broth into a clean saucepan and boil it down until it is reduced by half. Snip the string and carefully unwrap the veal, keeping it seam side down on the platter. Cut into 1½-inch-thick slices and arrange on a serving plate. Pour the reduced broth into a sauce dish and pass at the table.

IV

At Le Paquis

1936–1939

Prior to the Fishers' arrival in Vevey, Switzerland, Dillwyn had rented an apartment on the town square to accommodate the three of them until they could take up residence at Le Paquis the following year. For Al, the time living on the shores of Lake Geneva was a reminder of his earlier years abroad, and Mary Frances quickly got caught up in the excitement of the project to create an ideal place where she and Al could write, and where Dillwyn could paint. They purchased necessities—a car, kitchen utensils, foodstuffs, and wine—enjoyed the town's cafés and markets, ate delicious meals, and collected pieces of furniture that would later be used at Le Paquis. Dillwyn drew up architectural plans for the spacious house that he wanted to build around the original vigneron's stone hut.

Le Paquis was slightly below the small village of Chexbres, located in a little meadow that stretched along the terraced vineyards that rose above Lake Geneva in the appellation of St-Saphorin. The stone hut was famil-iar to the villagers because they had drawn water from its fountain for years, and the blooming of its meadows of wild asters, *les vendangeuses*, signaled the time of year for the grape harvest. An icy brook rimmed by willows ran through the property, and pear, plum, and apple trees bent away from the winds off the lake below.

Dillwyn planned to make the old stone hut the center of the new house. The original first-floor room would function as a reception area and foyer, with the old granite stairs leading to a combined study and bedroom for Mary Frances. Al's room and study were also part of the upstairs plan. A kitchen with two wide, deep windows was to be built a few steps above the spacious main room, and in it Dillwyn wanted to install shelves to display china, pewter, and cookbooks. According to his blueprints, a sink and gas stove would line one wall, and a collection of pots and pans would hang from the chimney. A window above the sink would provide light and fresh air. The main room would have floor-to-ceiling glass doors that opened onto a stone terrace, where meals could be served in summer. In winter, the fireplace in the main room would be the focal point that would draw guests together before they dined at a fine long table stretched along one side of the room. Throughout the living, dining, and kitchen areas, the aroma of cooking and the sounds of music and conversation could flow freely. Private studios and bedrooms would occupy the back and upper level of the house.

Dillwyn also designed three cellars to store the bounty of Le Paquis and the surrounding countryside. The first would hold jars of beans, tomatoes, vegetable juices, brandied fruits, and jams– products of the orchard and extensive gardens. This cellar would also be a cool place to keep salads and chilled desserts before they were served at dinner parties. The second cellar would have bins and slatted shelves for storing cabbages, apples, and root vegetables. The third would be a wine cellar, stocked with bottles produced by the local cooperative as well as older wines from Burgundy and eau-de-vie made from the fruit grown on the property.

In January 1937, the construction of Le Paquis began, and Al soon adopted the role of overseer of the project, which genuinely interested him and perhaps was also a ruse to escape what had come to be an over-

Le Paquis, above Vevey, Switzerland

crowded apartment. He and Dillwyn spent many hours planting a vegetable garden and sowing more wildflowers in the meadow. In mid-May,
even before the terraces were cleared of cement mixers and sawed beams,
and before the roof was finished or the windows installed, Mary Frances's
parents stopped at Vevey en route to Nice, where Rex planned to attend
an International Rotary conference.

A high point of their visit was a special picnic dinner when Mary
Frances served the first crop of peas on the terrace of Le Paquis. While Dillwyn, Al, and her father picked the peas and her mother shelled them, Mary
Frances boiled water over an open fire she had built among the bricks and
stones that still cluttered the terrace. After blanching the peas, she drained
off the water, swirled sweet butter and seasoning into the pan, and rushed

the dish to the picnic table. With the peas, they ate tiny roasted birds and warm baguettes from the village and drank chilled wine from the winery across the road. Rex was thrilled by the cow bells ringing a kind of mountain music, the pleasant al fresco meal, and the thin white wine from the local vineyard. Mary Frances remembered every moment of the experience, writing, "But what really mattered, and what piped the high unforgettable tune of perfection, were the peas, which came from their hot pot onto our thick china plates in a cloud, a kind of miasma of everything that anyone could ever want from them, even in a dream." Mary Frances had asked Al to remain in Vevey during her parents' visit, and he had agreed, although both of them realized that they would soon part. After her parents left for California, Al went to Strasbourg for the summer, and in the fall he accepted a teaching position at Smith College. Living under the same roof with two men who loved her had created an untenable situation, and Mary Frances had finally resolved it.

In the fall, when Dillwyn and Mary Frances took up residence in Le Paquis, she knew that the villagers quietly gossiped about their living arrangement, as did some of their friends who visited from the States, especially those who were close to Al. But the ambience of the house and her devotion to Dillwyn soon overcame any qualms she might have had about her role as mistress, and the all-too-brief year that she and Dillwyn lived at Le Paquis before they were forced to sell the property was an idyllic period that she could never repeat and would always remember.

Their lifestyle was also a source of curiosity to their neighbors and the villagers, who were not accustomed to seeing people of means doing so much of the gardening and cooking for themselves. Mary Frances and Dillwyn grew corn from kernels sent to them from the States. Mary Frances also harvested onions, garlic, and shallots, braided them into ropes, and hung them over the rafters in the attic. She learned from the Italian-Swiss villagers how to cook sweet peppers, eggplants, and onions in their own juices, flavored with butter or thick olive oil. Dillwyn fried tomatoes the way his family's cook had prepared them in Delaware. When alone, they dined on salads, ate corn oysters, freshly fried in butter, and drank glasses of beer cooled in the fountain.

The joy of purchasing fresh produce and other edibles in the market-places in Dijon and the preparation of simple meals in her first kitchen there more than five years before now developed into a lifestyle of growing, preserving, and fermenting the vegetables, fruits, and grapes harvested from their "little meadow." Although she did little writing at this time, Mary Frances told Larry Powell that she had contacted her editor, Gene Saxton, about doing a very personal book, because she felt her

At an outdoor market, Vevey, Switzerland, 1936

life had changed and become, in many respects, unfathomable even to herself.

During this halcyon period, Mary Frances and Dillwyn served their guests sherry on the terrace in the summer, followed by chilled soup or a casserole of small garden vegetables, which were cooked separately before being tossed together with sweet butter. Mary Frances ordered roasted chickens from the shops in Vevey and served them on a bed of herbs from the garden, sliced fresh bread from the local *boulangerie*, and poured *vin de pays*. In winter, the couple entertained in front of the fireplace and invited their guests to serve themselves from the large casserole simmering on the stove and from the salad bowl dominating the sideboard. First-time visitors pleaded for the name of the cook and were disbelieving when Mary Frances explained that she was the one who had made the ragouts and honey-baked pears she served.

During the last months of 1937, Mary Frances returned home to Whittier to tell her parents that she was divorcing Al. Whittier was still a small, socially conservative town, and her European gambol with Dillwyn undoubtedly inspired local gossip and caused embarrassment to the Kennedys. To Mary Frances's great relief, what she had thought would be the greatest obstacle to her happiness was overcome more easily than she had anticipated. Edith and Rex supported her decision unquestioningly. She was, consequently, unprepared for the eventual disapproval of Dillwyn's sister and mother, who showed their disappointment in small but hurtful ways.

On her return trip to Europe aboard the *Île de France*, Mary Frances became acutely conscious of reports of German aggression and the possible invasion of France. But she resolutely put the prospect of war out of her thoughts, refusing to entertain any suggestion that her days with Dillwyn at Le Paquis would end. Through the spring, the vines flourished

The Kennedy family, Whittier, 1937. From left: Rex, Mary Frances,
Norah, Edith, Anne's son Sean, Anne, and David.

and the meadow bloomed with violets, primulas, and crocuses. When summer arrived, the wildflowers grew waist-high, and the gardens yielded berries, onions, peas, and lettuces. Dillwyn's sister, Anne, and her poet friend came to spend the summer. And when Mary Frances's brother, David, and sister Norah arrived in Switzerland to study, they also visited Le Paquis.

Occasionally, Dillwyn and Mary Frances escaped the demands of the garden and summer guests and dined in the inns and restaurants that bordered Lake Geneva. They went to the Gasthaus zum Kreuz in Malters and to Hôtel des XIII Cantons in Châtel-St-Denis to savor impeccably fresh trout, and to Hôtel de Ville et du Raisin in Cully for sizzling platters of perch fillets. They also crossed the lake to dine and dance until dawn at the casino in Evian. But Le Paquis remained their refuge until

Dillwyn Parrish in the garden at Le Paquis, 1937

the fall of 1938, when events both global and personal shattered the world they had created in their "little meadow."

At the beginning of September, during a visit to Bern, Dillwyn suffered an embolism and sustained the amputation of one leg. In almost constant pain and virtually immobilized, he was told by his Swiss doctors that his condition was possibly a paralysis of the walls of the veins, which could only be treated by experimental drugs. And by the end of September, the Munich Agreement set the stage for war in Europe. Anne Parrish, David, Norah, and many of their friends left for the States, but Dillwyn and Mary Frances spent six months visiting various clinics in Switzerland, hoping to discover a cure but finding only medication for temporary relief. Unable to help Dillwyn with anything more than her presence, Mary Frances moved in and out of his pain-filled days and nights like a shadow, recording her own confused anguish in a journal.

They returned to California at the end of January 1939. Believing that the hot, dry air of the desert would be a tonic for Dillwyn's condition, they bought ninety acres of rocky land near Hemet, southwest of Palm Springs. And for legal reasons regarding property, Mary Frances became Mrs. Dillwyn Parrish in a civil ceremony in Riverside's City Hall. After the wedding they sailed back to France on the *Normandie* to procure medication available only in Switzerland and to arrange for the shipment of their things. Signs of war were everywhere when they crossed the border from France into Switzerland, but the accelerated pace of mobilization just served to counterpoint the slow pace of Dillwyn's physical deterioration. "The world seeped in. . . . [Dillwyn] was a man with one leg gone, the other and the two arms soon to go. . . . And I was a woman condemned, plucked at by demons, watching her true love die too slowly," she wrote. Less than a month later, they again boarded the *Normandie* to return to California.

Vevey Market Mushrooms
Adapted from *With Bold Knife and Fork*

While living near Vevey, Switzerland, Mary Frances patronized the local *marché aux champignons*, which took place once or twice a week during the season. Morels were plentiful, and the market also offered various mushrooms foraged from the forest and woods below the timberline of Mont Pelerin. This deceptively simple recipe for creamed mushrooms on toast will be greatly enhanced if you seek out wild mushrooms, rather than settling for their less interesting domestic cousins. *Serves 6*

1 quart mixed wild mushrooms such as porcini, chanterelle, fairy ring, and morel
4 tablespoons butter
1 shallot, finely chopped
1½ cups heavy cream
½ cup dry white wine
¼ cup chopped fresh chives, basil, or parsley
Salt
Freshly ground white pepper
6 thick slices French bread, toasted, buttered, and kept hot

Rub the mushrooms with a soft brush or a damp cloth to free them of soil. If using morels, rinse 6 times or more in cold water to cleanse, then separate the stem from the cap and check for insects. For other varieties, discard the stem if it is discolored, and halve or quarter large caps.

In a large skillet, melt the butter over medium heat. Add the shallot and mushrooms and stir while the mushrooms give off their juices. When most of the juices have evaporated, add the cream, wine, and chives and season with salt and pepper. Continue to stir until the liquid is bub-bling and slightly thickened and the mushrooms are tender; the timing will depend on the types of mushrooms you use.

Place a piece of toast on each plate and spoon the mushrooms and sauce over the top. Serve hot.

Petits Pois à la Française

Adapted from *How to Cook a Wolf*

Traditionally the glory of French "pea cookery," this dish of braised lettuce, peas, and onions can be made in a number of ways—all equally delicious. Mary Frances preferred the "cook fast in almost no water" method, rather than the more traditional braise, but admitted there were as many versions as there were good cooks. Serve the dish as a separate course with a well-chilled, not-too-dry Graves or rosé. *Serves 4 to 6*

½ cup water

1 head tender butter lettuce, coarsely shredded

6 green onions, white and tender green parts, cut into 2-inch-long
    julienne strips

¼ cup chopped fresh parsley

2 pounds peas, shelled

½ cup butter, cut in pieces, plus more to taste

Salt

Freshly ground black pepper

In a Dutch oven or other heavy pot, combine the water, lettuce, green onions, parsley, peas, and ½ cup butter. Cover, place over medium heat, and bring slowly to a boil, stirring occasionally. Lower the heat, and cook until there is almost no liquid and the vegetables are tender, about 5 minutes.

Season with salt and pepper and add butter to taste. Serve hot.

V

At Bareacres

1939–1949

Two buildings dominated the untillable hillside that Mary Frances and Dillwyn called Bareacres—a pine-board cabin that had once been owned by an outlaw Indian trader and a traditional Navaho adobe built for the woman who had followed him to Hemet Valley. When Dillwyn and Mary Frances purchased the property, both buildings were stripped and empty. No trace remained of the "squaw man" or Navaho woman except a bullet hole in the south window of the main house that was a reminder that he had been murdered, but their sad legend lived on in the valley.

Located a thousand feet above a dry riverbed that separated the rocky hills and canyon-split terrain from the apricot groves of Hemet Valley, the cabin was in vivid contrast to the vigneron's hut nestled in the meadow high above Lake Geneva. But of necessity, Mary Frances and Dillwyn immediately began the practical renovation of their hillside home, although in a different mood and with a different purpose than for their romantic creation of Le Paquis.

With the help of two old carpenters and a plumber, they added two baths and a guest room, and they screened the two porches to provide a studio for Dillwyn in one wing of the house and an outdoor sleeping porch

Bareacres, in Hemet, California

in the other. In the sheltered space between the two wings, they laid a stone patio, bordered on the south by a waist-high stone wall. French doors from each wing and a Dutch door from the kitchen opened to the patio, which they furnished with tables, chairs, and two chaise longues. This open-air room served as an outdoor kitchen for grilling, a favorite dining space, and, occasionally, a bedroom under the stars.

The kitchen, with its views of the San Jacinto Mountains to the east, was more spacious than Mary Frances's former kitchens. Built over an old cement porch, its floor was covered with patterned linoleum, and it was equipped with a porcelain sink, a white enameled stove, an icebox, and ample counters, shelves, and bins. Mary Frances also hung a mirror in an old mahogany frame on the wall next to the door so she could add a touch of lipstick or smooth her hair before she answered a knock on the door. And an old three-legged stool proved to be the right height to sit on while grinding coffee beans or shucking corn.

Mary Frances sought out the local purveyors of meat, poultry, and eggs in Hemet and Riverside, preferring to shop in small proprietor-owned stores rather than in the growing number of larger, more impersonal markets. Although not harvested in her own garden, the produce Mary Frances served was the finest that California could offer, and the straight-forward simplicity of her meals continued to reflect the influence of months spent on the rue Monge and the year at Le Paquis.

At Bareacres the Parrishes dined simply, eating their meals either on the patio or at a dining table near the imposing stone fireplace in the living room. When they entertained, they typically served a first course of

Dillwyn Parrish at Bareacres, 1941

chilled marinated green beans and tomatoes or other seasonal vegetables, followed by an entrée of rare steak or curried lamb with Indian rice. A compote of fresh or preserved fruits usually concluded the meal. When they dined alone, Mary Frances prepared a cheese soufflé with a light salad or broiled lamb chops garnished with herb butter or scrambled eggs with toast. Depending on the menu and the mood, they drank either wine or ale.

But as the months passed, their days of relaxed meals and leisurely conversation increasingly became a foil to the anxious and pain-filled nights that had come to dominate their lives. Neither the doctors at the Mayo Clinic, where Dillwyn was diagnosed with Buerger's disease, nor Mary Frances's own trusted physician, Dr. Hal Bieler, could offer hope of a cure; there was only the specter of more amputations.

During his last year, Dillwyn painted with furious intent, using every-thing from still-life subjects to live models to inspire his broad-stroked canvases. At the same time, Mary Frances staked out more territory in the "humanistic-gastronomic writing" that she had pioneered in *Serve It Forth*. Once again, her new project was suggested by culinary history, memories of childhood, and a series of remarkable meals. When she and Dillwyn visited New Orleans on their way to spend Christmas with Dill-wyn's mother in Delaware, they ate oysters on the half shell on Bourbon Street and oysters Rockefeller at Antoine's restaurant. At a small tavern in Delaware, Mary Frances watched an experienced bartender concoct the best oyster stew she had ever tasted. Her stories about these and other oyster-savoring experiences and her revisions of legends about the androgynous bivalve not only distracted and pleased Dillwyn but also be-came the first book in which she blended both recipes and narrative into a seamless whole.

Ironically, Mary Frances's copy of *Consider the Oyster*, which she had dedicated to Dillwyn, arrived in Hemet only a few days after his suicide on August 6, 1941. "I remember that I wrote a sad little criticism to my new editor, Sam Sloan, of Duell, Sloan & Pearce, about how I wished that I'd been notified earlier that the book would be published, because nei-ther [Dillwyn] nor I knew about it and I very mistakenly felt, for a few minutes anyway, that he might have put off dying, if he'd known the publication date. As it was, he never saw the book," Mary Frances wrote later in one of the few references that she ever made to the death of her lover and mentor a month after her thirty-third birthday.

Deep in grief and debt-ridden after her husband's suicide, Mary Frances stayed intermittently at both her parents' ranch and at Bareacres. And at the urging of her family she joined her sister Norah, their brother, David, and his young wife, Sarah, in Chapala, Mexico, where the three were painting murals in the public baths and trying to decide what to do with their lives. The trip proved to be salutary. En route to Guadalajara, Mary Frances had dinner in a stopover hotel, and the satisfying meal of beans and tortillas she ate awakened her appetite for the first time since Dillwyn's death. The comfort food of her childhood and the street food that was a part of Southern California living had worked their magic.

She also found that the change of scene and living with her younger sister, brother, and sister-in-law lifted her spirits. In the small kitchen of their rented house, she washed the lettuces, tomatoes, and radishes that she purchased in the market in Guadalajara and boiled eggs for their informal lunches, although the local dishes of guacamole and chicken enchiladas and the music of the mariachi bands lured them out to the cafés for their evening meals. As the days passed, Mary Frances began to observe David's strange fascination with the mariachi band's soloist, Juanito, and his inexplicable remoteness from Sarah, and she found it unsettling and felt a strange foreboding.

They returned to California on the eve of Pearl Harbor. The United States declared war on Japan on December 8, and the West Coast armed for a possible invasion. Norah, David, and Sarah took up residence at the Ranch, while Mary Frances divided her time between staying at her sister Anne's apartment in Beverly Hills and Bareacres. Drawing on her experience in Europe during the early days of World War II, she began publishing articles on food rationing and coping with shortages in Rex's *Whittier News*. Continually refining her ideas about meals and the preparation of food in times of scarcity and bomb shelters, she started her next book, *How to Cook a Wolf*, and wrote convincingly about how to survive the devastation of war and death. She had experience with both.

The recipes Mary Frances collected in *How to Cook a Wolf* provided insights into the culinary convictions she had developed from her childhood days, her coming of age in Dijon, her gardening and cooking months at Le Paquis, and most recently her time at Bareacres. Her dismissal of the "three squares" regularly recommended in women's magazines prompted her to spell out her own alternative: a balanced day rather than a balanced meal, because "balance is something that depends entirely on the individual. One man, because of his chemical set-up, may need more proteins. Another, more nervous perhaps . . . may find meats and eggs and cheeses an active poison, and have to live with what grace he can on salads and cooked squash."

For breakfast, she suggested buttered toast with jam or honey, and milk or coffee. In cold weather she recommended nutty porridge with raisins or chopped dates and maple syrup. She thought that fruit juice and coffee served together were pure poison, but juice at midmorning was a great pick-me-up. Rather than a lunch of tomato soup, beef patties, mashed potatoes, lima beans, Waldorf salad, and Jell-O—a combination that was frequently touted in newspapers and magazines as an "ideal" meal—she advocated "an enormous salad . . . or a casserole of vegetables, or an ample soup, plenty of buttered toast, wine, milk, or tea."

She included recipes for southern spoon bread and tomato soup cake as well as instructions for *petits pois à la française* and *fruits aux sept liqueurs*. The various chapters, although heavily embellished with autobiographical vignettes, also stressed cooking techniques—how to cook an egg, bake a loaf of bread, concoct a bowl of soup—and offered sage advice: "A smoother, thicker, richer soup will result if a liaison of egg yolk added to a little cream or stock is stirred into the soup just before serving. . . . Herb butters make any kind of meat and fish taste better than it was meant to. . . . One thing to remember about cooking any fowl, whether wild or domesticated, is that a good scrub with a cut lemon, never water, will make it tenderer and will seal in its flavors. . . . No vegetable should be cooked as long as you might think."

How to Cook a Wolf was written in under three months during the winter of 1942, and Mary Frances said, "It seemed quite natural to do a good book exactly as I would do a good report for Father's paper, to earn my living in the only way I could. This was probably the first time I was aware of writing to pay my way, and it may have helped keep everything so clear and fast."

There were pauses in her solitary Bareacres routine when she tried to supplement the income from her writing with various short-term jobs, but it was only when William Dozier hired her as a part-time junior scriptwriter at Paramount Pictures in May that she rented a one-room apartment in Hollywood. In July 1942 *Look* magazine featured M. F. K. Fisher in its series on successful career women. The Hollywood-style photos that accompanied the article portrayed Mary Frances at Paramount, shopping for melons and bread, grinding her own coffee beans, and tending her six grapevines at Bareacres. The article and, especially, the photographs introduced a woman who was not only an acclaimed writer but also a very glamorous and confident woman who knew her way around Hollywood.

Initially, she had accepted invitations from Gloria Stuart, an old friend from Laguna Beach, to dine at her home in the Garden of Allah, and invitations to mingle with producers and actors at studio cocktail parties. But she also grew accustomed to preparing easy meals and eating by herself after a long day of script writing. She shopped for fresh eggs on the way to work, always had a can of tomato soup at the ready, and bought a case of wine. Using a small hot plate, she scrambled eggs and heated soup that she garnished with a dash of sherry. She drank a glass or two of wine while dining, and completed the meal with a pear and a wedge of Teleme Jack cheese.

Because dining in memorable restaurants had always been an important part of her life, Mary Frances disliked the practice of combining din-

With a baker, photographed for a Look *magazine profile, 1942.*
Photo by Earl Theisen.

ing and business that was so much a part of the Hollywood social scene. She also considered each person's ordering and eating a different meal to be uncivilized, because there were too many aromas, too many tastes, and too many distractions from the waitstaff for the meal to achieve the harmony that she thought important. Above all, she felt the split focus on business and pleasure ruined the spirit of breaking the same bread and drinking the same wine and leisurely conversing for hours in cele-bration of a special occasion.

When she did feel obliged to share a meal with her friends and asso-ciates, she developed her own special way "to entertain" them at one of her favorite restaurants, because her apartment was too small for a din-ner party. "I telephoned the restaurant the day before and asked for a table in accord with my friend's local importance. This obviated standing in line, which is ignominious. . . . Then I ordered the meal and . . . by or-dering in advance I avoided another horrible barrier to decent dining out: the confusion that inevitably follows the first showing of menu cards . . . the third thing I did was see the headwaiter and tip him . . . and I finally arranged for the bill to be mailed to me. . . . When I walked out of the restaurant I felt that I had done everything I could to assure my friend of a meal which I could have given him for one-fourth the cost and about one-eighth the bother at home."

During the war years Hollywood was a fascinating place to live and work. Actors, screenwriters, producers, and musicians who had fled Europe contributed to the quality of motion pictures. The major Holly-wood studios supported the war effort and assigned actors, directors, and screenwriters to special units to help by documenting troop movements, producing propaganda films, entertaining the troops, and promoting the sale of war bonds. So it was not implausible when Mary Frances told fam-ily and friends that she had been given a "secret mission" in April that would take her away from Hollywood to an undisclosed location until August 1943.

In reality, she was five months pregnant, and she took up residence in a boardinghouse in Altadena to await the birth of her first child. After Anne Kennedy Parrish (who later changed her first name to Anna) was born on August 15, Mary Frances introduced her baby to her family as an adopted daughter and never revealed the identity of the girl's father. With the help of a Hemet woman who served as a nursemaid for Anne, Mary Frances took up residence at Bareacres and eventually decided to leave Paramount Pictures.

While at the boardinghouse, Mary Frances had written *The Gastronomical Me*, a work that detailed the events and sea changes that had contributed to her gastronomical coming of age. Using a phrase from George Santayana—"the measure of my powers"—as the title for many chapters in the book, Mary Frances retold a series of vivid autobiographical scenes that together revealed the story of her life, including the role that her grandmother played in her childhood, the impact of her adolescent adventures, and the story of her first marriage and her affair and subsequent marriage to Dillwyn. She concluded the book with the Mexican trip that had raised questions about her brother's instability and foreshadowed his suicide only a few months after he returned from Lake Chapala. To readers who had come to expect lighthearted stories, rollicking culinary history, and recipes from M. F. K. Fisher, *The Gastronomical Me* signaled a watershed. Not only was it her most personal book to date, but, according to reviewers, it was also her finest.

The success of *How to Cook a Wolf* had led to a contract to write a series of articles for *Coronet*. The publication of *The Gastronomical Me* in late 1943 led to contracts to write for *Harper's Bazaar* and *House Beautiful*. Mary Frances's magazine articles introduced a literary tone into food journal-

ism and anticipated a time when wine would be as integral to home entertaining as it was to fine restaurant dining. In the *House Beautiful* se-
quences, especially, Mary Frances wrote about seasonal holidays and
time-honored events, suggesting food and wine to serve "in honor of
spring," on the Fourth of July, at Thanksgiving, and at Christmas. The
House Beautiful articles also described wedding luncheons of *coquilles aux
crevettes* rather than the customary chicken à la king, and Christmas oysters with sauce vinaigrette instead of the usual blast of horseradish and
ketchup. A Bacchus cocktail set the theme for a Valentine's Day lunch that
included a salad of Belgian endive and Parma violets. And a spring menu
recommended stuffed oysters paired with a good Chablis or Grey Ries-
ling before the r-less months signaled the end of the oyster season.

In April 1945, when the events of the war and lingering grief over both
Dillwyn's and David's suicides as well as her own financial uncertainty
weighed heavily on her, Mary Frances decided to escape to New York City
for a few months with Anne and her nursemaid. Invited to a friend's cocktail party during her first week there, she met an oft-married, now di-
vorced former publisher and agent, Donald Friede, who seized the moment and asked her to lunch that week. With a May breeze blowing over
the café table, she shared a bottle of Louis Martini's Folle Blanche and
ate a plate of *moules* more-or-less *marinières* with a man she would agree
to marry a few weeks later. After the precipitous wedding, Donald Friede
negotiated a summer lease on a duplex apartment in Greenwich Village
for his new wife, adopted daughter, and nursemaid.

During the early hours of the day, Mary Frances collected material in
the New York Public Library for a literary anthology called *Here Let Us
Feast.* In the late afternoons she drank white wine in the garden of the
Museum of Modern Art with Donald, and then they went to Park Avenue
or to the Village to party with his literary friends and associates. Because

With Donald Friede and their daughters, Bareacres, 1947

Donald had so many publishing contacts, Mary Frances's writing com-
mitments accelerated, and she added *Atlantic Monthly, Vogue, Town and
Country, Today's Woman,* and *Gourmet* to the list of magazines publishing
her work. With the encouragement of her new editor, Pat Covici, she
started a novel, *Not Now, But Now,* which Donald hoped would be picked
up by Hollywood and made into a movie. He also began talks with pub
lishers about a possible M. F. K. Fisher translation of Brillat-Savarin's
Physiology of Taste.

By the end of summer, Donald had decided to leave his position as a
reader and agent in New York City in order to write a memoir, and the
Friede family moved to Southern California to live at Bareacres. Within
a year, the high chair that Anne had vacated in the kitchen was occupied

by Mary Frances's second daughter, Kennedy Mary Friede, who was born seven weeks prematurely on March 12, 1946. Juggling her writing obligations and child-care duties, Mary Frances made nursery meals of chopped green beans, poached pears, whole wheat crackers spread with sweet butter, and milk. As she had done earlier with Anne, she expanded Kennedy's range of foods, giving her little tastes of an unknown fruit or vegetable, a flavored cracker, or a spoonful of kasha. "I myself was a fascinated witness to the first bite of so-called 'solid food' my elder daughter took . . . and felt that I was watching a kind of cosmic initiation to what, if I had anything to say about it, would be a lifetime of enjoyment of the pleasures of the table," she wrote. Then, after the children were fed and asleep, Mary Frances savored some of the most pleasant minutes of her day, when she changed into a kimono and shared a glass or two of sherry with Donald before eating a light dinner that might have been simmering on the stove or chilling in the refrigerator.

As a sophisticated man-about-town, Donald had a cultivated palate for fine wines and good food, especially the Russian dishes he had enjoyed during his childhood in Europe. So, when asked by his mother about the meals that his new wife, a woman of no small culinary reputation, served to him, his reply was an appreciative essay, "On Being Married to M. F. K. Fisher." In it he detailed the delicious vegetable or meat ragouts that cooked gently on the stove and filled the house with exciting aromas, and he also spoke of Mary Frances's fondness for leftovers, which always came to the table "twice as delicious, if that were possible, as they were in their original form. To my mind they are a perfect example of the triumph of an imaginative palate over the precise pages of a cookbook."

On weekends the Friedes usually entertained family or friends from Hollywood, and Mary Frances began to take notes on the phenomenon she had earlier called "marital gastronomy." In a journal devoted to the eating idiosyncrasies of family members and a few of the couples who were frequently her guests, she wrote about her mother's preference for the food of her Iowan childhood—baked fish, medium-cooked meat, rich desserts, hot breads, and pancakes. She also noted her father's fondness for traditional meals at home, but his bold taste for curries with multiple condiments, game, stuffed fowl, cheese instead of dessert, and strong coffee when dining away from home. Wondering what accounted for the many dissimilar taste preferences she had observed in the couples she knew, she sought explanations for various husband-wife gastronomic mismatches. Did the foods eaten during childhood or did later cosmopolitan dining experiences shape a person's tastes? Was the tendency she observed of men to like thick soups but not dips a reflection on gender roles? Or was there a subtle rebellion on the part of either spouse against the obliging give-and-take of domestic harmony? Although she found no satisfactory answer to these questions, the process of developing an educated palate remained a major culinary interest for her.

Mary Frances was an intellectual cook, mindful not only of her guests' food and drink preferences but also of her own role as a cook. In *With Bold Knife and Fork* she wrote of the different phases a cook might pass through during a lifetime. During one phase, she observed, the cook might concentrate on variations of favorite dishes, such as cold soups, noodles, or shellfish stews, and in another phase she might be interested in preparing vegetables in a number of different ways. She also observed how often a planned menu changed by the time it got to the table. Like her mother before her, she wrote menus in her yearly appointment book and then noted the dishes she actually served at a luncheon or dinner. She sometimes made menu changes based on what ingredients were available, or in response to some quirk she knew about a guest, but often she made a spontaneous change in a moment of inspiration.

The Bareacres kitchen was her space, and she chose to work in it alone. Perhaps she found the physical acts of peeling, chopping, mashing, and cooking to be relaxing after hours of writing in her studio, but those acts were also empowering. And the end result of exerting control over ingredients and processes was closely akin to her ability to arrange ideas and words into a poem, a story, an essay. The difference was, of course, that a well-made dish, unlike a well-crafted piece of writing, was short-lived. Still, there was creative energy in both and a certain amount of audacity. "A writing cook and a cooking writer must be bold at the desk as well as at the stove," she wrote, and she developed both her writing style and her cooking philosophy accordingly.

There were times, however, when Mary Frances departed from her solitary kitchen ways, as when she invited Norah and her two small boys to help with baking Pfeffernüsse cookies for Christmas. These holiday traditions were important to Mary Frances, and they often became the subjects of articles she wrote about entertaining during the holidays, even though her family baking sessions sometimes drove Donald to Hollywood or even farther from home.

Mary Frances's holiday projects, however, were not the only wedge driving her and her husband apart. Living in Hemet, Donald had developed health problems and had become increasingly unhappy with his career. He felt that he was stagnating at Bareacres: he was cut off from the wheeling-and-dealing world of New York publishing, unsuccessful as a Hollywood agent, and deeply in debt. He also had some difficulty in his role as a father, had definite ideas about raising his daughters, and remained a reluctant participant in children's pastimes. For her part, Mary Frances tried to keep her name in print and to insulate her children from their father, who felt that they should politely say, "Bonjour, Maman and Papa," and then disappear with a nanny. And she began to

question whether she would ever be able to resolve her domestic problems, which had been compounded by her mother's heart attacks and
death in May 1948.

Nine months later, Donald went for treatment to an expensive sana-
torium on the East Coast, leaving Mary Frances alone to raise their
daughters and to help her father cope with Edith's death. Near a nervous
collapse herself, she asked Donald not to return to California, convinced
that her third marriage was over. And soon, for all practical purposes,
her day-to-day life at Bareacres came to an end as well when she moved
to the Ranch with her daughters to keep house for Rex.

A Summer Salad

Mary Frances deplored the American custom of serving made-in-advance bowls of head lettuce, often doused with "Russian–Thousand Island–Roquefort" according to the customer's wishes, and was convinced that leafy green salads, simply dressed with oil and vinegar—and perhaps some of the meat juices from the steak or chicken platter—properly belonged after the main course. She also advocated what the French called *salades composées* (composed salads) as a main course, especially during the summer months. She said that she discovered the following salad of blanched vegetables in Venice, but the mild aioli dressing echoes her many years in Provence. *Serves 12*

AIOLI SAUCE
2 cloves garlic
3 egg yolks, room temperature
Salt
2 cups good-quality olive oil, room temperature
2 teaspoons fresh lemon juice, room temperature

SALAD
12 small zucchini, each 4 inches long, trimmed
1 pound haricots verts, tipped
1 pound small red potatoes
1 head cauliflower, separated into florets
24 canned anchovy fillets for garnish (optional)
Snipped fresh chives or minced fresh parsley for garnish (optional)

To make the aioli: crush the garlic cloves to a paste using a mortar and pestle. Add the egg yolks, one at a time, stirring with the pestle after each addition until the mixture is thick. Season with a little salt, mixing well. Transfer to a bowl and very slowly drizzle in the oil, beating constantly with a wire whisk until the sauce thickens. Slowly mix in the lemon juice. Cover and refrigerate until serving.

To make the salad: bring a large saucepan filled with salted water to a boil. Add the zucchini and boil just until tender, about 8 minutes. Drain, rinse under cold running water, and set aside. Separately cook the haricots verts, potatoes, and cauliflower florets in the same way, adjusting the timing as necessary.

Arrange the vegetables on 1 or 2 large platters. The zucchini can be halved lengthwise and each half garnished with an anchovy fillet. Sprinkle the vegetables with the chives. Serve the aioli in a bowl alongside.

Coquilles aux Crevettes
Adapted from *House Beautiful*

When searching for a menu for a light June wedding luncheon to recommend to *House Beautiful* readers, Mary Frances came up with this variation on coquilles Saint-Jacques. Using shrimp instead of scallops, she paired the creamed dish with tiny new potatoes, buttered and rolled in minced fresh herbs, to add just enough substance to a menu that began with a summer soup and ended with strawberry mousse and wedding cake. Champagne was served throughout. *Serves 8*

2 pounds shrimp, cooked, peeled, and deveined
1 pound mushrooms
6 tablespoons butter, plus 2 tablespoons, cut into bits, for topping
1 shallot, minced
4 green onions, white and tender green parts, finely chopped
3 tablespoons finely chopped fresh parsley
1 teaspoon salt
Freshly ground white pepper
6 tablespoons flour
1 cup dry white wine
3 cups chicken stock
½ cup heavy cream
1½ cups fresh bread crumbs

Preheat the broiler. If the shrimp are large, cut each one into 2 or 3 pieces. Rub the mushrooms with a soft brush or a damp cloth to free them of soil. Remove the stems and reserve for stock. Slice the caps.

In a large skillet, melt the 6 tablespoons butter over medium heat. Add the mushrooms, shallot, green onions, parsley, salt, and a sprinkling of pepper and sauté, stirring constantly to prevent browning, until the mushrooms give off their juices. Sprinkle the flour over the mushroom mixture and stir with a wooden spoon until the flour is absorbed. Remove from the heat and gradually add the wine and stock, stirring constantly. Return the pan to medium heat and cook, stirring often, until the sauce thickens, about 10 minutes.

Add the shrimp, stir in the cream, and heat briefly. Taste and correct the seasoning. Spoon the mixture into scallop shells or individual baking dishes. Sprinkle the tops with the bread crumbs, dividing them evenly, and dot with the 2 tablespoons butter.

Place the shells on a rimmed baking sheet and run under the broiler until the crumb topping is golden brown, a few minutes. Serve hot.

Brown Derby Hamburger

Adapted from *Coronet*

Mary Frances once said that she was a pushover for a prewar burger at a drive-in. But during her Hollywood days, she enjoyed the famous sirloin hamburger served at the Brown Derby, preferring it topped with mayonnaise, mustard, tangy relish, lettuce, and a slice of cheese. *Serves 6*

2 pounds ground sirloin
1 egg
1 cup concentrated chicken stock
2 tablespoons rendered chicken fat
2 tablespoons Worcestershire sauce
½ teaspoon English mustard
1 tablespoon salt
1 teaspoon freshly ground black pepper
6 hamburger buns, split and toasted

In a bowl, combine the meat, egg, and stock. Mix in the chicken fat, Worcestershire sauce, mustard, salt, and pepper. Divide the mixture into 6 portions and form into patties. Cover and refrigerate for at least 30 minutes or up to several hours.

Preheat the broiler or prepare a fire in a grill. Broil or grill, turning once, to the desired degree of doneness. Serve the burgers on the toasted buns.

California and Provence

1949–1961

After moving the children with their toys and pets into the Ranch in November 1949, Mary Frances tried to attend to the house, which had been neglected during Edith's prolonged illness the last few years. She spruced up the interior by painting and wallpapering, sewing new curtains, making a playroom for her daughters in the master bedroom, and creating an office in her bedroom. She made some necessary changes in the kitchen by installing a children's table so Kennedy and Anne could gather there while she cooked. She also made an effort to prepare Rex's favorite dishes and invite his friends and associates to meals, and to provide a gathering place for her sisters and their families.

Now the resident gardener, housekeeper, cook, and, as her father's health deteriorated, nurse, Mary Frances found herself working in the kitchen of her youth, the scene of some of her fondest memories of her mother and of the good, wholesome food she had eaten as a child. She added a freezer to the cookhouse, planned nourishing meals for the family, and devised ways to juggle her busy schedule and the preparation of seasonal foods. "And what is here before me?" Rex would ask mockingly, but in an appreciative way, as he lifted a pot lid and saw carrots, potatoes, or cauliflower simmering on the stove. And he slyly urged every-one to finish the food on the table to stay Mary Frances's deft hand with leftovers. In "From A to Z," she wrote, "I think of myself dining with my father, such a strangely relaxed, amicable meeting after the years of family confusion at table."

The holiday traditions she had participated in during childhood had come full circle for her. She orchestrated cookie baking, arranged pine boughs, poured special wines, and prepared favorite dishes for her sis-ters and their families at the Ranch. She called on her tallest nephew to string the lights on the Christmas tree; she coaxed the youngest cousin into peeling blanched almonds for the Christmas cake. When her father's brothers visited from Michigan and Spokane, they praised the care that Mary Frances provided for Rex.

Gradually, however, the demands of life at the Ranch—helping her father edit the *News*, relying on paid household help, preparing meals (even welcoming the availability of Minute Rice), and chauffeuring her daughters to school—left Mary Frances harried, distracted, and too weary to write anything more than a short magazine article. When her bouts of sleep deprivation and anxiety became too unnerving, she sought help from a psychiatrist in Los Angeles and came to rely more heavily on the advice of Dr. Bieler.

Long a physician to Hollywood stars like Gloria Swanson and Gloria Stuart, Dr. Bieler emphasized the importance of phytonutrients in the diet, warned about the ill effects of sugar, and believed that the cause of disease was not germs but toxemia. Although his first book, *Food Is Your Best Medicine*, was not published until the mid-1960s, he had been ad-dressing all kinds of ailments with specific nutritional approaches long before that, and he had prescribed various diets for Mary Frances and her children. Diagnosing Mary Frances with a potentially toxic liver, he

Rex Kennedy, 1959

The Red Cottage, south of St. Helena, California

strongly recommended that she eat vegetables, especially zucchini, as often as possible, supplemented by an occasional raw egg. During most of her adult life, she privately followed this diet.

When Rex Kennedy died on June 2, 1953, Mary Frances and her sisters decided to sell the Ranch and the newspaper. Rather than return to Hemet, Mary Frances rented out Bareacres and moved to Northern California because of the lure of wine country. As a child, she had visited the small wineries that stretched from San Gabriel to San Diego with her father and sampled a bit of Italian-Swiss Colony Tipo Red from his glass. Twenty years later, she and Dillwyn adapted the cycle of planting and harvesting grapes to their lives in Vevey, and they had enjoyed the fruit of their labors. Now Mary Frances was determined to raise her daughters among the vineyards of Napa Valley, where she rented a house called the Red Cottage on Sulphur Springs Avenue south of St. Helena. Living in a house of her own again was an opportunity to unpack her books, hang Dillwyn's paintings, and become acquainted with neighbors who had children the ages of Anne and Kennedy. The kitchen became a gathering place where Kennedy and Anne ate cookies and told their mother about Girl Scout meetings and their classes at school, and where the people who wrote wine newsletters, designed wine labels, and made wine could meet and sample the latest vintage. The cottage on Sulphur Springs Avenue also became the scene of family holiday celebrations when Norah and her sons rented a cottage nearby before settling into their new home in Berkeley.

After her first year there, however, Mary Frances began to feel that the education that she envisioned for her daughters would probably necessitate dividing months and even years between the small town that was their new home and older places in a much older world. So Mary Frances decided to spend her share of her father's estate to give her daughters the cultural advantages of living in Europe and learning another language. In August 1954, they moved out of the Red Cottage and sailed for France, where Mary Frances planned to visit Paris with her daughters, perhaps rent Le Paquis for a time, and take up residence in Arles. But Georges Connes, a friend and her former professor in Dijon, warned her about the severity of the mistral in Arles and urged her to consider Aix-en-Provence instead.

A month later Mary Frances, Anne, and Kennedy walked from their hotel in Aix toward the splashing fountain named in honor of King René, located at the east end of the Cours Mirabeau. Before them "the green tunnel of the Cours stretched westward . . . more like a flashing vision of promise than any yet seen." At the Deux Garçons café the little girls sipped lemonade while Mary Frances drank an aperitif "in complete and sudden ease: we were in the right place at the right moment, and we knew it would last." A leisurely lunch at the Glacier restaurant at the other end of the Cours set the pattern for their almost daily visits to their "two havens" on the Cours Mirabeau.

In order to practice conversational French during their first months in Aix, Anne and Kennedy boarded with Madame Wytenhove and her four children in an apartment facing the Place des Martyrs de la Résistance. They also attended St. Catherine's Dominican School as day students with the Wytenhove children. Mary Frances rented a small room in the home of Madame Lanes on the rue Cardinale, and once again she found herself a pensionnaire in the home of an upper-middle-class woman who had been impoverished by war and who bowed to having strangers share her rooms and table.

During the week, Mary Frances met the children at the school door after classes and had an aperitif with them at the Deux Garçons before she accompanied them to the Wytenhoves' apartment and returned to Madame Lanes's for her own evening meal. On some days, she and her daughters dined in a restaurant, where they became acquainted with a very savvy dog they called Boss Dog, because he seemed in command of the roving canines and knew his way around some of the best kitchens in town. During their many months of observing the comings and goings of the dog with one stand-up ear and one floppy ear, Mary Frances began writing a book for her daughters. Focusing her story on the antics of Boss Dog, who strutted his stuff in and out of the markets and who frequented the Glacier, Madame Paoli's, and the Deux Garçons, Mary Frances attempted to capture something of the magic of the Provençal city she and her girls had grown to know and love.

On weekends, Mary Frances, Kennedy, and Anne spent time on the rue Cardinale and had lunch at Madame Lanes's table. They frequently attended a matinee and then stopped at a café, where the girls drank hot

chocolate and Mary Frances enjoyed a snifter of cognac before they returned to their respective lodgings. Occasionally, they took weekend trips
to explore Avignon, or they followed Cézanne's route on long walks from
the center of Aix through the pine woods and vineyards. The day before
Christmas, they boarded a bus for Marseille, where their room at the
Hôtel Beauvau looked out over the historic Old Port and down onto the
quai des Belges.

From the fall of 1954 until spring, Mary Frances and her daughters
studied, wrote, and dined in quarters not their own. And then, quite by
accident, they found themselves with a home in the country. Although
only a few months remained before they would return to California, Mary
Frances was able to rent a renovated apartment above the stables of the
Château du Tholonet. Located about five miles east of Aix, the château
was surrounded by poppy-studded meadows and pine-covered slopes.
While the children spent most of their days outdoors in the company of
an old shepherd and his flock, Mary Frances prepared food in the first
of her many kitchens in Provence.

Unlike her *petite cuisine* on the rue Monge in Dijon, this kitchen had
a fourteen-foot ceiling and a large window that overlooked the countryside. The walls of the nine-by-nine room were whitewashed stone, the
floor was covered with red tile, and an old pine table stood in the center
of the room. In the space where three grates and a hood had once served
as a grill for stable boys, a small white butane stove stood on a red-tiled plat-
form. A shallow hollow in a slab of local stone served as a sink, drained
by a simple pipe that emptied into the courtyard below. Two borrowed
pans and a skillet provided minimal cookware, and the serving bowls,
plates, and casseroles were green and yellow glazed Provençal pottery, a
distinguishing feature of her later kitchens as well.

Mary Frances shopped for daily foodstuffs in the bountiful markets

Le Tholonet, Aix-en-Provence, France

in Aix, which had tempted her during her months of boardinghouse meals. She made the trip to the market three times a week, and she observed how the availability of produce was inexorably dictated by the calendar, as strawberries gave way to cherries and green peas were replaced by little purple artichokes. Since she had no refrigeration, Mary Frances knew that acquiring the freshest produce meant she would have to race against time in order to prepare and serve a meal before the natural process of decay would prevail. But the superior taste and quality of fresh food made frequent trips to the market worthwhile. And she took comfort in the fact that if a fish spoiled or a tomato rotted in the interval between lunch and supper, there was always a can of sardines, anchovies, or lark pâté to satisfy hunger.

With the sensitivity of a still-life artist, Mary Frances would arrange the clay water pitcher, the wine bottles, and a wicker tray of vegetables and lemons on the pine table, where in the morning they drank large bowls of café au lait and ate slices of Dijon gingerbread with butter and Alpine honey, just as she and Norah had done years earlier on the rue Monge. She also prepared picnics of mild cheeses, fresh bread, green olives, and little radishes to be eaten in the meadows on warm sunny days. When the mistral blew over the fields, they ate their lunch of sliced ripe tomatoes or boiled new potatoes dressed in sweet butter in the kitchen. Writing about a meal of a single vegetable with butter and a glass of milk, Mary Frances observed, "One can't eat that way with others to feed—although the children and I often managed it in the country, in

Provence and California. It dictates a simplicity we've had to grow away from." And her daughter Kennedy recalls "running down our hill to the shepherd's home and bringing back warm milk for my mother. She would make us clabber custard, and I still dream of the thick, rich, sweet dessert on my tongue."

After years of shopping for groceries in California's chain stores, Mary Frances found that purchasing soft-boiled eggs from the shepherdess, salad greens from the farmer, and fresh seafood from the traveling fishmonger who stopped at Le Tholonet every Friday made living good in that wild, beautiful country only five miles away from the dignified town homes of Aix. When the time came to pack and say good-bye, she felt it was too soon, just as she had almost fourteen years earlier, when leaving Le Paquis was a weight upon the heart.

Mary Frances and her daughters left Provence early in July 1955, accompanied by the sixteen-year-old Wytenhove daughter, Monique, who had decided to continue high school in the States, and Norah and her two sons, who had joined their aunt and cousins at Le Tholonet in June. After an arduous crossing on the freighter *Vesuvio*, they landed in San Francisco. Mary Frances picked up her new yellow station wagon, collected trunks, suitcases, and boxes at the pier, and drove her extended family to an apartment that her sister Anne had rented for her in the "Van Ness Gulch" of the city.

Mary Frances's experiment in city living was difficult and short-lived. After a day of classes in the local public school, young Anne attended the San Francisco Ballet School and Kennedy studied the flute. Monique attended Lowell High School and took extra lessons in English. Mary Frances chaperoned their comings and goings while maintaining a busy writing schedule. Life became a series of humdrum appointments, and there seemed little time to enjoy the theater, art exhibits, and restaurants

With her daughters and nephews in Avignon, 1955. From left:
David Barr, Anne, Mary Frances, Kennedy, and John Barr.

The Dear Old Lady, on Oak Avenue, St. Helena, California

that San Francisco offered. Frustrated that the children could not play or ride their bicycles or experience the freedom they had grown used to at Le Tholonet, Mary Frances decided to sell Bareacres, bank the proceeds, rent a place among the vineyards, and as quickly as possible find a house in St. Helena to purchase.

In the late summer of 1956, about six weeks before Monique returned to Aix, Mary Frances bought an old Victorian house in St. Helena. Built around 1869, the Dear Old Lady, as they soon came to call the house, proved to be the perfect place to accommodate Mary Frances's daughters, relatives, and friends, as well as the Girl Scouts, 4-H clubbers, and members of the St. Helena community who took an interest in wine or literature.

The three-storied, mustard-colored house was on Oak Avenue, one block west of the main street in St. Helena. Originally home to one of the Italian winemakers in the valley, the house was half hidden by masses of Peking bamboo, leafy trees, and shrubs that etched shadows on the architectural detailing of the attic gable and the Victorian woodwork framing the front room's bay window. Inside the house there was an unusual mixture of light and color caused by the bamboo leaves tracing delicate, curtainlike patterns on the tall windows of the first floor. The kitchen and enclosed porch on the west side of the house opened to a lovely yard, perfect for outdoor dining. The Mayacama Range, which separated Napa from the Sonoma Valley, stretched into the distance.

A living room, office, two bedrooms, bath, kitchen, and sun porch occupied the main floor, and the attic, which ran the length and width of the house, was reserved for Mary Frances's bedroom and for storage space. Because the first floor was well above ground level, the old house also had a spacious basement, which Mary Frances converted into living space. With the help of Boy Scout volunteers and professional workmen, she added a half bath and several small, wide windows to brighten the area, which had a stone foundation, whitewashed stone walls, and a wine cellar she called a pub. The renovated basement became an ideal place for entertaining guests as well as a cool place to write during the hot summer months.

The kitchen was located between the living room and the sun porch. The walls were dark green, outlined in white woodwork; the cupboards were stained wood; and all of the appliances were white. The dark brown table in the center of the room could seat ten, but Mary Frances usually preferred to have six or eight guests dine comfortably around it. She also hung one of her favorite pieces of art, a Braque reproduction that reflected the various colors in the room, above a long bookcase opposite the kitchen counter.

Friendships Mary Frances had made when she lived at the Red Cottage continued to flourish around the kitchen table on Oak Avenue. Organizations such as the Napa Valley Wine Library came into being over a meal of rare roast rib of beef and Beaulieu cabernet. When the Junior Players Club finished rehearsing their current play in the makeshift theater that the Dear Old Lady's garage had become, there were always pitchers of milk and juice and plates of cookies laid out on the table for the hungry thespians. Kennedy and Anne brought their friends home for meals, and Anne remembered her mother's cooking as "simple, unfashionably simple and good. (She would serve salami, prosciutto and melon, a big salad of romaine, crisp sourdough, and good wine. Maybe some grapes or ice cream for dessert. My friends were baffled, but always came back for more)." And when the summer heat became unbearable, Mary Frances and her daughters carried trays of deviled eggs, salads, cheeses, and wine downstairs to the pub for an evening party.

The lure of the Old World persisted, however, especially since Mary Frances was finding it difficult to cope with the adolescence of her older daughter in California. Hoping to recapture something of the simplicity she and her daughters had enjoyed in Aix five years earlier, Mary Frances made plans to return to Europe in the fall of 1959, to introduce Anne and Kennedy to another language and another country. Influenced by Paco Gould, a publicist for Krug wines, and his Italian-born wife, Romi, they made Lugano, Switzerland, their destination, and Mary Frances enrolled the girls in Santa Anna, the same convent boarding school that Romi had attended. After searching the possibilities of lodging for herself, Mary Frances rented a pleasant room in the home of Signora Donati and her husband, a retired journalist from whom she arranged to take Italian lessons.

During the fall Mary Frances spent a week in Dijon visiting Georges Connes and attending the yearly Foire Gastronomique to gather material for an article she was writing for *Holiday* magazine. But when she returned to Lugano, she found that the weather had turned bone-chilling, and the damp winds off the lake caused spells of coughing that were not relieved by the various medications prescribed for her.

When Donald and his new wife and publishing partner, Eleanor Friede, arrived to spend the Christmas holidays with Mary Frances and the girls in Paris, Anne and Kennedy welcomed their vacation from school, and especially from Lugano. And when they left Paris for a stopover in Aix-en-Provence, the city of splashing fountains worked its magic again. Mary Frances decided to return to Aix after the girls' classes at Santa Anna were over in the spring. Three months later, she rented a few rooms in a farmhouse called L'Harmas three miles outside of Aix-en-Provence on the route du Tholonet. Her dreams of lying in a meadow filled with wildflowers became a reality. Basking in the early spring sun and drinking herbal teas that her daughters made for her cured the cough that had plagued her during the past months in Lugano. Revived in body and spirit, she concentrated her attention on reading, writing, and cooking.

Her second kitchen in Provence was a small room equipped with a tiny Frigidaire, a modern white enameled stove, a hollowed-out old marble sink, shelves, and two windows that opened to a terrace shaded by trees. On the large kitchen table she placed baskets of beans or peas that needed stringing or shelling. Because the refrigerator could hold only small quantities of meat or fish, she converted a little room that had once been a buttery into an impromptu storeroom. Several hooks in the stone walls of the room were perfect for hanging bags of eggplants, onions, potatoes—any vegetable that did not have to be cooked immediately. Using the top of a broken piano as a shelf, she stored bowls of fresh fruit, trays of ripe tomatoes, and a crock of sweet butter.

Three times a week, Mary Frances walked into Aix to shop and returned in a taxi with baskets and string bags filled with provisions for the next two days. She found that six years had made a subtle difference in the city and in the friends she knew there. Madame Lanes seemed younger and somewhat freer from the constraints of postwar living. There were fewer physically broken people in public; more students crowded the cafés on the Cours. But Ange, their favorite waiter at the Glacier, had faded, as had the Glacier itself. Only the city's markets were unchanged. On Tuesday, Thursday, and Saturday, the big food and flower markets attracted the townspeople with stalls displaying fruits, vegetables, herbs, poultry, meat, fish, sausages, and cheeses of every kind. The flea market in front of the Place du Palais also lured both dealers and the curious, who rummaged through the *brocante*.

At L'Harmas, their large living room also served as a dining room, but Mary Frances often varied the setting for a meal depending on the season. In cool weather she and her daughters ate by the fire in the living room; in spring, the terrace was warm and ankle-deep in wildflowers and grasses, a perfect spot for reverie with plate and glass in hand. In the heat of summer, they ate by the bowed shutters in the kitchen, which kept the room cool against the blaze of white dusty heat. And when the early autumn breezes began to blow, Mary Frances often carried her meal to the pine forest and dined with a tree for a backrest.

In late September, when school began again for Anne and Kennedy, they reluctantly moved from L'Harmas to the top floor of the Hôtel de Provence on the rue Espariot. It was a friendly hotel owned by the Segond family, who lived in an apartment on the first landing and rented rooms to their friends and to long-term lodgers. Mary Frances and her two daughters chose a suite of rooms on the top floor. Anne had a small room with a window that opened to the sounds of the fountain in the Place d'Albertas, and Mary Frances and Kennedy shared the large room that served as living room, study, and bedroom. Its three windows looked out onto rooftops and down into an apartment across a narrow street. Because there was not even a makeshift kitchen, they ate most of their meals in the cafés and restaurants that were well known to them.

Possibly because Anne and Kennedy were so familiar with the beautiful old city and so practiced at balancing days of study with relaxed evenings, they attended all of the exhibits at the Musée Granet, mingled with the crowds at the Carnaval d'Aix, and saw *Don Giovanni* and other musical events at the famous summer festival. These were precious days for Mary Frances, but they were passing too quickly. While she knew that when she walked in the direction of La Rotonde, "my children would be waiting for me under the faint returning green of the trees on the Cours," she also knew that the next time she visited this ancient city, they would, undoubtedly, not be with her. Anne was already planning the celebration of her eighteenth birthday in August.

During the 1950s, while food additives, fast-food restaurants, anything-but-white kitchen appliances, and ever-larger supermarkets came to dominate the American scene, Mary Frances and her daughters had lived for extended periods of time in the south of France. There they cooked in minimalist kitchens in renovated shepherds' stables and artists' quarters. The photos of the U.S. vice president showing off modern kitchen appliances to the Soviet premier that appeared in *Le Monde* in 1959 provided Mary Frances with a startling commentary on the American concept of an ideal kitchen. She had embraced the challenges of preparing delicious meals with ingredients purchased in the outdoor markets of Aix and Marseille and was convinced that savoring a simple supper of bread, cheeses, fresh vegetables, and local wine could be as satisfying as an elaborate meal prepared in an up-to-date home kitchen or enjoyed in a two- or three-star restaurant. And she wrote about her kitchens in Provence with a sense of supreme satisfaction and nostalgia.

Private-Method Zucchini
Adapted from *With Bold Knife and Fork*

Mary Frances sometimes referred to this zucchini dish as her own private, comforting mishmash, and often enjoyed it as a main course when dining alone or with a chosen few. An "innocent dish," it was a staple of her diet, first prescribed by Dr. Hal Bieler. *Serves 6 to 8*

10 small zucchini, trimmed and quartered lengthwise
5 small summer squashes, trimmed, halved lengthwise, seeded,
    and quartered
2 stalks celery, trimmed and thinly sliced
¼ cup chopped fresh parsley
4 green onions, white and tender green parts, thinly sliced
Butter, at room temperature
Salt
Freshly ground black pepper
Buttered toast for serving

In a large saucepan, combine the zucchini, squashes, celery, parsley, and green onions and add enough water to cover the vegetables. Bring to a boil, reduce the heat to a simmer, and cook, uncovered, until the vegetables are tender, 8 to 10 minutes.

Drain well, return to the pan, and mash with a potato masher until smooth. Add butter, salt, and pepper to taste. Serve hot in warmed bowls accompanied with buttered toast.

Summer Savory Soup

Adapted from House Beautiful

"Most people, especially men, seem to feel safer with a thick soup than a thin one," M. F. K. Fisher wrote in *With Bold Knife and Fork*. But she also conceded that it was nice sometimes to have a "pitcher of a clear broth when people are standing around and talking after a concert or after a meeting of Puzzled Moms and Dads, Ltd." This deep-toned clear soup is an admirable choice for late summer, when fresh tomatoes are abundant. *Serves 8*

10 tomatoes, cored, quartered, and lightly mashed
1 onion, finely chopped
8 cups water
1 teaspoon chopped fresh summer savory
6 white peppercorns
1 teaspoon sugar
1 teaspoon salt
1 bay leaf
12 small, young beets
3 carrots
3 stalks celery with leaves
2 eggshells, crushed
2 egg whites, lightly beaten

In a saucepan, combine the tomatoes, onion, 2 cups of the water, and the summer savory, peppercorns, sugar, salt, and bay leaf. Bring to a boil, reduce the heat to a simmer, and cook gently until the tomatoes are cooked, about 30 minutes. Remove from the heat, pass through a fine strainer, and set aside.

Meanwhile, in another saucepan, combine the beets, carrots, and celery in 6 cups of the water, bring to a boil, and boil until the vegetables are tender, about 15 minutes. Strain the liquid into a large saucepan and discard the solids.

Add the tomato liquid to the mixed-vegetable liquid and let cool completely.

Add the eggshells and egg whites to the soup, place over low heat, and heat, stirring constantly, until the soup comes to a boil. Boil for about 1 minute. Remove from the heat and let stand for about 20 minutes.

Line the strainer with a double thickness of cheesecloth, and place over a clean saucepan. Push the scum on the surface of the soup to one side, and ladle the soup through the strainer. Reheat but do not allow to boil, then taste and correct the seasoning. Serve hot in consommé cups.

Gnocchi Zucca

Adapted from *With Bold Knife and Fork*

When Mary Frances and her daughters lived in Lugano in 1959, Anne and Kennedy boarded at a convent school to learn Italian and pursue their studies. Mary Frances rented a room in a house nearby, where she also took Italian lessons and shared the evening meal with Signora Donati della Pietà's family. This dish is a re-creation of the signora's pumpkin dumplings. *Serves 4 to 6*

2 cups fresh or canned pumpkin puree
2 eggs, lightly beaten
½ to 1 cup flour
½ teaspoon baking powder
½ teaspoon ground nutmeg
½ teaspoon salt
1 teaspoon freshly ground white pepper
1 teaspoon olive oil
2 tablespoons butter, cut into bits
Fresh sage leaves, fried in butter until crisp, for garnish (optional)

In a bowl, mix together the pumpkin puree and eggs until blended. Gradually add ½ cup flour, baking powder, nutmeg, salt, and pepper and stir well, adding more flour as needed to create a smooth, slightly sticky dough. Set aside for about 1 hour.

Preheat the oven to 350 degrees. Butter a shallow baking dish.

Bring a large pot of salted water to a boil and add the oil. Working in batches, drop the dough by teaspoons into the water. Lower the heat to a simmer. When the gnocchi rise to the surface, after about 5 minutes, cook for 30 seconds more, then, using a slotted spoon, transfer to a colander to drain.

When all of the gnocchi are cooked, arrange them in a single layer in the baking dish, and dot with the butter. Place in the oven until the tops are glazed, about 15 minutes. Crumble the sage leaves over the top, if desired, and serve hot.

Tomates Farcies à la Provençale

Nothing says Provence more provocatively than midseason tomatoes stuffed with anchovies, capers, fresh herbs, and bread crumbs. They were a particular favorite of Mary Frances's because they could be served either hot or at room temperature and served as a side dish with either an omelet or a more substantial lamb chop or steak. *Serves 8*

4 large tomatoes

STUFFING

2 tablespoons olive oil or butter

2 tablespoons minced onion

1 clove garlic, minced

2 tablespoons chopped fresh parsley

1 tablespoon drained capers

2 thick slices sourdough bread, crusts removed, quartered, moistened
   in beef stock, and squeezed dry

3 salt-packed anchovies, well rinsed, filleted, and mashed to a paste

¼ cup fine dried bread crumbs

¼ cup olive oil

Preheat the oven to 375 degrees. Lightly butter or oil a shallow baking dish.

Slice each tomato in half through the equator. Gently squeeze each half, forcing out the juice and seeds, then scoop out the pulp into a bowl. Discard the juice and seeds. Cut the pulp into small pieces. Invert the tomato shells on absorbent paper to drain.

To make the stuffing: heat the 2 tablespoons oil in a saucepan over medium-high heat. Add the onion and sauté until lightly browned, about 5 minutes. Add the tomato pulp, garlic, parsley, capers, soaked bread crumbs, and anchovy paste, stir well, cover, and cook over medium heat until the liquid from the tomato pulp evaporates, about 10 minutes.

Pat the inside of each tomato shell dry, and arrange the shells, hollow side up, in the baking dish. Divide the stuffing evenly among the tomatoes. Top the stuffing with the dried bread crumbs and moisten with the ¼ cup oil.

Bake until the crumbs are golden and crisp and the tomatoes are cooked through but still firm, about 35 minutes. Serve hot, warm, or at room temperature.

VII

In St. Helena

1961–1970

In July 1961, Mary Frances, Anne, and Kennedy left Aix-en-Provence for the short trip to Marseille and the longer journey to San Francisco and St. Helena. The summer was more than half over, and planning for the next phase of her daughters' education was uppermost in Mary Frances's mind. While in Aix, Anne had contacted Donald Friede to request information about acting schools in New York, and he had made preliminary arrangements for classes and housing for her. With two more years of high school to complete, Kennedy was destined to remain at home with her mother and attend the local school in St. Helena.

After a gala birthday party in August, Anne left for New York, and after Labor Day, Kennedy began classes. Gathering her notes about Aix, Mary Frances started to write a book about the magical city that had been the scene of so many of their planned gatherings and chance encounters. But by midyear, health problems began to plague her, and she was forced to endure extensive tests to diagnose a condition her physicians agreed was a collagen deficiency. To her dismay, Mary Frances also discovered that the course of study at the local school was not challenging enough for her younger daughter. Rather than jeopardize prospects for a planned career in medicine, she transferred Kennedy to a private boarding school in Menlo Park. For the next six months Mary Frances divided her time between an apartment in Berkeley and weekends with Kennedy in St. Helena. She also visited her sister Anne and her husband in Genoa, Nevada, which to her surprise reminded her of the rugged terrain at Bareacres, and she felt at ease with the people who traded and farmed in that desolate niche on the Immigrant Trail.

When Kennedy graduated in 1963 and decided to enroll in a premed program at Russell Sage College in Troy, New York, Mary Frances's immediate domestic responsibilities were literally over. The house in St. Helena, with its spacious kitchen and now unoccupied bedrooms, continued to be an important part of her life as well as a safe depository for her books, Dillwyn Parrish's paintings, various pieces of furniture that had been in her family for generations, and remnants of her former homes in Vevey and Hemet. But now, with both her daughters on the East Coast, she found herself leaving the large old house to write in places that seemed right at the moment, and preparing meals in make-do kitchens that somehow inspired articles even as they challenged her culinary skills.

After a family gathering during the holidays in December 1963, Mary Frances announced that she had volunteered to teach at an African American boarding school in Piney Woods, Mississippi, during the summer and fall of 1964. Certainly the civil rights movement was a strong motivation in her decision, but so was her curiosity about life in the South and about a well-known school that had been attracting retired teachers and academics from the North for years. Although her students were eager to learn, the experience was not a happy one. To her chagrin, she found that neither the dominating attitude of the dean of students nor the starch-heavy diet at the school was congenial to her. Further complications arose when she discovered that Anne was pregnant and fleeing New York for Berkeley. Believing that her responsibility was to help her daughter, she decided to leave the school before the end of the fall semester with a promise to return the following summer. But in January 1965, the administration informed her that, despite her success with the students, she would not be invited back to teach during the summer months.

Behind her casual comments in letters to her family and friends about not being asked to return, there was a sense of frustration that her efforts had accomplished so little. The Piney Woods experiment had shaken her confidence, and her complex relationship with her older daughter revealed what she had come to believe were her shortcomings as a caring mother. She even wondered whether there was a future for the kind of writing that had brought her success in the past. Since the beginning of the sixties the focus of the best American cookbooks had changed from collections of recipes to books that had themes and explored the cuisines of other countries. Recognizing this, the *New Yorker* had enlisted Mary Frances as not only a knowledgeable food authority but also a seasoned writer to do a series of cookbook reviews, and her agent, Henry Volkening, negotiated a contract with the *New Yorker* while she was still at Piney Woods. Mary Frances rose to the challenge.

Her house in St. Helena was rented, and Berkeley, where Norah had assumed the care of Anne, was not a viable alternative because of the difficult relationship that had developed between Anne and Mary Frances. So she retreated to the house next door to her sister Anne's home in Genoa for a period of uninterrupted work. Although the cottage was difficult to heat and most of the food available from the local grocery store was packaged or frozen, it was amusing if difficult to cook there. She told

Anne's cottage, Genoa, Nevada

Kennedy how she "skinned" frozen scallops of their bread coating, sautéed them lightly in hot butter, and served them with rice, and how she crumbled Ranger cookies and mixed them with brown sugar and butter to prepare a crust for an apple tart. Rather enjoying the obstacles the old-fashioned kitchen presented, she cooked nourishing meals for herself, often dined with her sister and brother-in-law, and worked well in that solitary landscape.

Despite the fact that Mary Frances succeeded in publishing three major articles in the *New Yorker* in 1965 and became a grandmother when Anne delivered a handsome son, Jean-Christofe Chanderli, in March, the year was also marked by further estrangement and sorrow. Mary Frances was still exiled from Berkeley, her former husband, Donald Friede, died suddenly in May, and her sister Anne passed away in August after an unsuccessful gastrointestinal operation. Whatever their differences, the bond between Mary Frances and her sister was a strong one, and Anne's death affected her deeply, as did Donald's. As their daughters grew older, Mary Frances had come to think of him and his fifth wife, Eleanor, as friends and confidants, and his passing left a void in her life and an intense desire to return to Provence, where she had experienced happy holidays with both her sister and her former husband, and even happier days with her two daughters.

In 1966, an offer from the book division of Time-Life to write the text of *The Cooking of Provincial France*, the first volume in the Foods of the World series, gave Mary Frances an opportunity to return to France. In Paris, she spent most of her time with the Time-Life staff and with a young Frenchwoman, Annie Boulat, and her family, who had been selected to represent a typical family who lived both in Paris and in a country cottage forty miles south of the capital. In Paris, Annie routinely shopped in the local street markets and prepared meals in her small, cheerful kitchen overlooking the boulevard du Montparnasse. During weekends and holidays in the country, she and her family visited a nearby farm to purchase fresh vegetables they picked themselves. While her husband and children hunted for girolles in the woods and gathered raspberries from their own bushes, Annie would spend the day making a tart and preparing a *potée*. Photographers documented these scenes as well as delightful moments when the family gathered for an outdoor lunch around their picnic table in the country and more formal occasions when the Boulats entertained guests in their Montparnasse apartment.

Mary Frances wove the family's story into a text that concentrated on the eleven historic provinces of France and their notable contributions to the country's cuisine. She also described the pattern of the typical French meal. Usually served in the middle of the day, and often called *dîner*, the meal began with an hors d'œuvre, which could be anything from fresh radishes with bread and butter to truffled goose pâté. The main course would be fish, meat, or fowl. A *petite salade* of garden lettuces followed the entrée, and a cheese course and dessert completed the meal.

Impressed by the way such multicourse dinners were prepared in kitchens that Americans would consider underequipped and too small, Mary Frances praised contemporary Frenchwomen for doing most of their own cooking, unlike women of previous generations, who had employed servants to do it. She described how remodeled kitchens in France now had either gas or electricity for cooking, modern appliances, and, in some cases, dishwashers. Still, one remnant from the past dominated even the most up-to-date kitchens: a traditional wooden table in the middle of the room remained the focal point and the place where the family gathered to eat.

The Time-Life research trip also took Mary Frances to Provence. She visited Aix during the music festival, celebrated her fifty-eighth birthday in Marseille, and stayed in Julia Child's home, La Pitchoune, in Plascassier, together with Michael Field, the consulting editor for the volume, and his wife. Although Mary Frances liked the former concert pianist, who was now a famous cooking school instructor, she simply couldn't understand why he planned to learn about Provençal food by visiting two- and three-star restaurants rather than researching the local ingredients. She was also amazed to discover that Julia's kitchen, with its professional equipment, was virtually unused by Michael and his wife. They had no interest in cooking, they had no inclination to test recipes that were indigenous to the area, and they stocked the refrigerator with iced vodka and dried salamis rather than with the distinctive products of the Côte d'Azur. Still, Mary Frances regarded the trip as a great plus in her life, coming at exactly the right time and focusing her attention

In the Dear Old Lady kitchen, St. Helena, circa 1957

on that part of the world that always made her feel more herself than any other place. The resulting book, *The Cooking of Provincial France*, became her first foray into the professional culinary world, and it initiated a friendship with professionals such as Julia Child, Simone Beck, James Beard, and Judith Jones.

When not in France, Fisher resided in St. Helena. The kitchen in her Victorian house doubled as a dining room, and she enjoyed serving meals to her family, friends, and other writers and culinary associates who sought her out. During her years in the Napa Valley, she also actively supported the production of quality wine in the valley, gave lectures on wine and food pairing, and helped to found the Napa Valley Wine Association. Long an advocate of wine with meals, Fisher loved living among the vines, and she loved sharing her table with winemakers and those involved in the production and promotion of local wines. Proud of not owning a television set, Fisher paid no attention to the increasingly popular cooking shows, and she reviewed cookbooks for the *New Yorker* in her own whimsical way, seeking out the off-beat and showing little patience for the growing number of recipe collections that featured trendy foods, sixty-minute meals, and restaurateurs. In the seventies, when cooking literally became an art form and dining as a social grace was taken seriously, entertaining often and serving fine food were signs of living well. Kitchens became the gathering places; professional appliances became status symbols. But Mary Frances had little time and even less patience with trends.

Her contract with the *New Yorker* and the regular publication of her articles in that magazine had greatly enhanced her literary career, and *The Cooking of Provincial France* had opened doors into the food establishment, but it was an agreement with Putnam to publish her favorite recipes that positioned her in the middle of the cookbook scene that developed in the late sixties and seventies. At the urging of her editor, William Targ, Mary Frances agreed to collect the "tried and true" recipes that she had tucked into books or scribbled in the notebooks that filled the bookcases of her kitchen. And the *New Yorker* negotiated the right to excerpt ten chapters, under the title "Gastronomy Recalled," before the publication of the book, which she called *With Bold Knife and Fork*, in 1969. Beginning on September 7, 1968, Mary Frances's essays on hunger and enjoyment, secret ingredients, pickling, innards, rice, and casseroles—interspersed with recipes—appeared in the magazine. What readers discovered embedded within the essays, however, were memories of nursery meals, comfort foods, and special feasts, complete with recipes that were literally autobiographical notes, jottings from a lifetime.

Although Mary Frances had enjoyed many successes during the sixties, the decade had also brought much disappointment and pain into her life. She had spent most of her inheritance, supplemented by contributions from Donald Friede, on giving her daughters what she deemed the best education possible, but she had not prepared herself for the decisions they would make when they grew up. Anne lost interest in dance and the theater, became a part of the Berkeley hippie scene, and was eventually diagnosed as having bipolar disorder. For several years she either involved her mother in her problems or rejected all help and advice, drifting from relationship to relationship and from place to place. Kennedy's choice of husband and his antipathy toward her mother and extended family of aunts and cousins also caused more pain than Mary Frances cared to admit. But Mary Frances continued to organize holiday gatherings in St. Helena in an effort to draw her sister, nephews, in-laws, children, and grandchildren together. She was generous to a fault, and at times it seemed that she was "trying to run an unlicensed but popular motel-bar-restaurant there instead of the welcoming warm home my girls and I had lived in for a long time." Still, her hospitality never wavered, until she imagined herself being found on the kitchen floor of the too-large house on Oak Avenue with a glass of champagne and a half-eaten pear on the kitchen counter. This image reinforced her worst fears about living alone, and Mary Frances began to seek out other options in other places.

Captain Jansson's Temptation

As her yearly appointment books revealed, this casserole was a standby in M. F. K. Fisher's kitchen, especially during her last years in St. Helena. Reputed to be the creation of a Finnish Captain Jansson, an ascetic person who preached abstinence and self-control during the fin de siècle, the delicious casserole of potatoes, onions, anchovies, butter, breadcrumbs, and cream proved to be his one weakness. Another legend links the dish to a traditional Swedish Christmas meal. Whatever the origin, Mary Frances may have learned about it when she and her daughters visited some wealthy friends in Sweden on their way back to California from Aix in 1961. *Serves 6*

5 baking potatoes, peeled and cut into ¼-inch-thick slices
One 2-ounce can oil-packed flat anchovy fillets, drained
1 large Spanish onion, cut into ¼-inch-thick slices
2 cups heavy cream
¼ cup dried bread crumbs
¼ teaspoon freshly ground black pepper
Bibb lettuce leaves for serving (optional)

Preheat the oven to 350 degrees.

Place the potato slices in a buttered 11-by-7-inch baking dish. Layer the anchovy fillets on top, and then cover with the onion slices. Pour the cream over the layers, and sprinkle with the bread crumbs. Grind the pepper over the top.

Cover with aluminum foil and bake for 30 minutes. Uncover and continue baking until the potatoes are tender and the top is lightly browned, about 45 minutes longer. Serve hot, on a bed of lettuce leaves, if desired.

Clam Mousse

Adapted from *House Beautiful*

In the late 1960s, when Mary Frances was reviewing the recipes in her "tried and true" file while preparing *With Bold Knife and Fork*, she also made note of the staples on her pantry shelf. Bottled clam juice and cans of minced clams were high on her list. And although she did not include the recipe for this mousse in the shellfish chapter, "How to Spring Like a Flea," she had offered it to readers of *House Beautiful* years earlier as a first course to a dinner that featured highly flavored curry as the main course. She recommended serving it in chilled glass cups, to be put at each place setting just before calling the guests to the table. *Serves 8*

2 cups bottled clam juice
2 cups chicken stock
1 envelope (2½ teaspoons) unflavored gelatin
Tabasco or West Indian hot-pepper sauce
1 egg white
1 cup heavy cream
Chopped watercress or snipped fresh chives for garnish (optional)

In a saucepan, combine the clam juice and stock and bring just to a boil. Remove from the heat. Ladle ½ cup of the hot liquid into a small bowl and stir in the gelatin until dissolved. Stir the gelatin mixture into the remaining clam juice and stock. Mix in a few drops of pepper sauce. Pour into a large bowl and let cool completely.

In another large bowl, whip the egg white until stiff peaks form. In a medium-sized bowl, beat the cream until stiff peaks form. Fold the whipped cream into the egg white just until combined. Then fold the combined mixtures into the gelatin mixture. Cover and refrigerate for 2 to 3 hours, stirring often, until the mousse is well chilled and a soft texture has developed.

Spoon into chilled glass cups or shells. Serve garnished with the watercress, if desired.

VIII

Last House

1971–1980

When her friend David Bouverie offered to build Mary Frances a house on his ranch, which was two miles from Glen Ellen in the Valley of the Moon, she felt uneasy about giving up the house on Oak Avenue with its nine beds, spacious kitchen, and good neighbors, but the beauty, security, and privacy provided by five hundred acres of meadows, streams, and foothills were tempting. And she did look forward to the wonderful blend of solitude and camaraderie she expected to find at the Bouverie Ranch. In her letters to her family she described the prospect of living in a two-room house there as an exciting new phase of her life. Although she admitted being horrified at the thought of having to settle on the details of what would be her last kitchen, when she was given the opportunity to specify the design of the house, she made three requests. She wanted two rooms and a big bath, black-tiled floors throughout, and an arch at each end of the house that would repeat the curve of the ranch's barn doors. David Bouverie, an architect as well as a rancher, incorporated her wishes into the working plans.

The house with its vaulted redwood ceilings was built into a slope, with living areas on two levels. Mary Frances's bedroom and a low terraced balcony were on one level, three feet higher than the living room and a second balcony that looked westward to the mountains of Jack London State Park. The bedroom with its eastern exposure was not as spacious as the living room, but it was cozy and perfect for writing, reading, and sleeping. Sliding glass doors led to both balconies, and when Mary Frances opened the windows, the house was filled with fragrance from the nearby groves of madrone, eucalyptus, and bay.

The entrance to the house was a cool, bookcase-lined foyer that led to Mary Frances's room, the bathroom, and the steps down to the living room. Every detail reflected a flair for the dramatic. Recessed bookcases throughout the house held Mary Frances's personal library of over five thousand volumes, which were shelved by genre. In the bathroom, which was painted Pompeian red and tiled in a Moroccan design, original sketches by Picasso, paintings by Dillwyn Parrish, and a changing exhibit of lithographs, cartoons, and portraits gave visual delight to the bather who wished to contemplate them from the oversized tub.

Because Mary Frances's work and sleep patterns were so interconnected, one room accommodated both activities well. She read late into the night, preferred to write very early in the morning, and in the afternoon liked to nap or leaf through manuscripts on her bed, which she covered with a big purple bedspread that she liked to say was woven by witches in Haiti. Remembrances of the past were everywhere in her bedroom—her grandfather's revolving bookcase, an ancient portrait of Ursula von Ott, a print of "The Seven Ages of Man," and a box of faded photographs.

The main room in Last House, where Mary Frances cooked, ate, and relaxed, was designed for moments of solitude as well as for entertaining. Cabinets, a stove, counters, a sink, and the refrigerator occupied the south wall. Three windows stretched above the sink and counters, and a

Last House, near Glen Ellen, California

bookcase was at a right angle to the refrigerator. A dining table surrounded by comfortable chairs filled the corner, and a wood-burning Franklin stove was installed in an alcove in the east wall. A couch, chaise longue, upholstered chairs, and various tables occupied the rest of the room.

Mary Frances kept a glass vase or an old pitcher filled with flowers on the antique Swiss refectory table, and she continued the tradition she had begun in Aix of decorating with still-life arrangements of seasonal fruits and vegetables. Old and new cookbooks, novels, mysteries, and reference books lined the north wall, and the bookcase behind the dining table contained an assortment of plates, pictures, and well-used copies of the two volumes of Julia Child's *Mastering the Art of French Cooking*, Irma Rombauer's *Joy of Cooking*, the *Larousse Gastronomique*, and Escoffier's *Guide Culinaire*. She liked to say that she took ideas from all of them and

then prepared the kind of food inspired by the immediacy of the moment or the weather within and without.

Undoubtedly, during the early 1970s the weather within and without was variable, as Mary Frances went through spells of contentment at Last House alternating with spells of restlessness. Although she compared the first two years of living at the Bouverie Ranch to being "a guest in a delightful rented cottage perhaps there to write a book, to hide, to escape," she slowly grew into the place and came to feel she belonged there. Nevertheless, she was careful to balance her time in the Valley of the Moon with visits to more familiar landscapes.

Provence—with its ancient stones, splashing fountains, bountiful markets, and Old World ambience—drew her like a magnet. Unlike her former home in St. Helena, Last House was easy to leave because the ranch was staffed with reliable help and the property was well protected. Mary Frances also acquired an enthusiastic traveling companion when Norah retired and joined her on trips. In 1970, 1973, 1976, and 1978, they spent several months in La Roquette, Marseille, and Aix, where their writing and research projects often paled in comparison to their adventures in living and preparing meals in their impromptu kitchens. "The one in Marseille in 1973 was perhaps the least dignified of any of a long lifetime of them," Mary Frances wrote, describing the makeshift kitchen located in the bathroom. They set up a two-burner gas hot plate beside a miniscule washbasin, a soup pot shared a shelf with toothbrushes, and a sagging string held both face and dish towels. But the two large rooms they had rented in Marseille were airy, and they dined at a table under a big window that looked down on the Old Port. While Norah went to the Abbaye de St-Victor in the morning to research the life of Mary Magdalene, Mary Frances wrote in her bedroom and prepared a simple soup, a fish stew, or vegetables in a vinaigrette sauce for the midday meal. Occasionally, they dined in one of the restaurants in the narrow streets near the Old Port, but more often than not they stayed in their rooms, where they opened a bottle of the local vin rosé, set the table with their newly acquired Provençal pottery, ate local cheeses, pâtés, and salads, and enjoyed the miracle of good plain wine and food.

Three years later, Mary Frances and Norah decided to make Aix-en-Provence their home for several months. On the rue Brueys, two short blocks from the Cours Mirabeau, they rented a large, pleasant room with a kitchen alcove and a large dressing room. Although minimal, the kitchen did have a stove, a small Frigidaire, a sink, and some counter space. And they had easy access to the incomparable fruits and vegetables of the Aix market to sustain them. "We had perhaps four pans and kettles, and could braise little quails for a treat, or make a lusty ratatouille, or even a dainty omelet," Mary Frances wrote when describing their kitchen. The only disagreeable aspect of their room was the noise of motorcycles racing down the rue Brueys from early morning until late at night.

Like every kitchen in Provence that Mary Frances had adopted as her own, this one offered a distinctive culinary experience and served to expand her views about not only what to eat but also how to eat. The alchemy of bouillabaisse served in a wild-mustard-colored soup tureen, the secrecy surrounding a recipe for *calissons,* and the charity of a "nursery tea"—Mary Frances was able to translate all from Old World to New for her readers because she had made the journey herself.

In April 1978 Mary Frances flew with Norah to New York City, where she received the Grande Dame Award from the New York chapter of Les Dames d'Escoffier. They then flew to Marseille for a one-month visit to Aix, Le Tholonet, and the Childs' home in Plascassier. On the sunny patio of La Pitchoune, Julia served her houseguests battered deep-fried zucchini blossoms, boned and stuffed chicken, mesclun salad, and cheeses—all beautifully paired with wine from Paul's cellar. The nearby markets of Nice offered fresh vegetables and seafood, olives bursting with flavor, and local dishes such as *socca.* When Norah and Mary Frances dined in restaurants, they savored young spring lamb, spit roasted and basted with its own flavorful juices. But there were other aspects of the trip that were not so idyllic. Mary Frances had developed arthritis, which limited her walking, and the country air at Le Tholonet caused her to develop a hacking cough. Proud and not wanting to be a burden to Norah, she welcomed the flight that took them from Nice to San Francisco

Fearful that long-distance travel would become increasingly difficult, if not impossible, Mary Frances had more or less resigned herself to living life as fully as possible at the Bouverie Ranch when she received an

Julia Child at La Pitchoune in Plascassier, 1972. © Estate of Horst P. Horst. Courtesy Art + Commerce.

offer she could not refuse. Her longtime friend and Japanese culinary authority, Shizuo Tsuji, asked her to write the introduction to *Japanese Cooking: A Simple Art*, and he invited her to Japan to immerse herself in the country's cuisine. Taking Norah as a companion, she flew to Osaka on October 1 and kept a detailed journal of the various accommodations and restaurants they visited in Osaka, Kobe, Kyoto, and Tokyo. She also recorded observations about the private classes they took with Tsuji and his chefs, as well as the multicourse luncheons they enjoyed at his school and at the various markets they toured.

The two-week introduction to Japanese *ryori* was transformative. Never before had Mary Frances experienced the visual excitement of so many unfamiliar meats, types of fish, and vegetables or the elaborate symbolism of such delicately sculpted ingredients. She observed classes on tempura, sashimi, and dashi, sampled udon, and sat at traditional low tables for eleven- and twelve-course dinners. She also wrote to her friends that she could live on raw fish and rice for the rest of her life. But the positive feelings she had about her culinary experiences were under-cut by reservations about the cultural and societal differences between East and West, especially what she observed to be the subservient role of women in Japan.

When she returned to California, she continued to drive over the Oakville Grade to St. Helena to see her friends and her dentist, doctor, and CPA. But she also had made many friends among the winemakers and shopkeepers in Sonoma, and the social life on the ranch, especially when David Bouverie was in residence, kept her occupied as a hostess to many of his events as well as her own entertaining. With ranch people nearby to keep a friendly eye on her, Last House not only safeguarded her privacy but also was a perfect place to cope with the various physical handicaps that developed after 1978.

Arthritis, drastically changing vision that eventually necessitated eye surgery, throat problems, and the onset of Parkinson's disease demanded adjustments in her lifestyle. Good friends chauffeured her to San Fran-cisco for art exhibits and theatrical performances; she hired a secretary not only to type her manuscripts but also to help her with correspondence and bills. Knowing her fondness for the movies of Marcel Pagnol, Alice Waters brought reels of his films, a projector, and a picnic supper from

Chez Panisse. Other friends in the culinary community, like Chuck Williams, Julia Child, and James Beard, brought special treats such as fresh crab from Fisherman's Wharf for an evening of good food, wine, and gossip. A letter or a telephone call usually ended with an invitation to Last House, only an hour from San Francisco. And there was always an article to be written, an interview to be given, and a book nearing completion.

While the meals that she had prepared and served in St. Helena presented Mary Frances in her essential role as a gracious hostess, the meals she served in the kitchen-dining-living room at Last House became a distillation of all the years of simple, make-do meals she had prepared in many other places—flavorful soups, blanched vegetables, seasonal fruits gleaming in their natural syrups. These dishes, along with the wines of the Valley of the Moon, were the staples of her table as she found yet simpler ways to entertain.

There were, however, certain constants in her cooking that she never abandoned in favor of time-saving devices. She was particular about the texture of the soups she prepared, and she avoided blenders and Cuisinarts even though they were offered to her. Instead, she used a *tamis* to achieve the consistency she desired. She preferred a mortar and pestle to crush biscuits for scalloped oysters or clams and to blend Moroccan *chermoula*, a dish of green and red peppers bonded with olive oil, garlic, and coriander. But she did bow to a few modern conveniences, and she stocked her pantry with a selection of fine preserved and imported foods. She had used a freezer since housekeeping for her father in Whittier, and at Last House she froze loaves of sourdough wheat bread from a family of Basque bakers in the village of Sonoma. She usually kept thin slices of smoked salmon prepared in nearby Petaluma by an Eskimo friend, blueberries from Alaska macerated in brown sugar, and jars of shucked Tomales Bay oysters in her refrigerator.

Eventually, capricious eyesight, untrustworthy legs, and a hip replacement operation virtually prohibited any more forays into the distant places that remained nostalgically present in her writings. Limiting her travel to California, she made the Stanford Court Hotel her home away from home, and room service a substitute for her kitchen. Jim Nassikas, who liked to entertain the culinary elite at his hotel, filled her room with flowers, fruit baskets, and champagne. James Dodge, the pastry chef at the Stanford Court, baked croissants, brioche, and special tarts for her, and she always visited the kitchen to praise the chef.

But Last House increasingly became her refuge and the place most closely associated with the persona she had created. "It is very simple: I am here because I choose to be," she wrote. "I move about fairly surely and safely in my *palazzino*, and water the plants on the two balconies. I devise little 'inside picnics' and 'nursery teas' for people who like to sit in the Big Room and drink some of the good wines that grow and flow in these northern valleys. I work hard and happily on good days, and on comparatively creaky ones I pull my Japanese comforter over the old bones . . . and wait for the never-failing surcease."

Quail Ragout

These tiny game birds were always a favorite roasting and braising item for Mary Frances. She often stuffed them and gave a brace to friends for their holiday enjoyment. This recipe is a version of the classic coq au vin.
Serves 4

8 quail
2 cups chicken stock
8 slices bacon, diced
1 sweet onion, chopped
2 carrots, peeled and chopped
2 stalks celery, trimmed and chopped
4 cloves garlic
12 mushrooms, brushed or wiped clean, stems trimmed,
    and caps quartered
2 tablespoons flour
2 cups dry red wine
3 tablespoons chopped fresh parsley
1 tablespoon red currant jelly
1 tablespoon brown sugar
2 teaspoons fresh thyme leaves
Salt
Freshly ground black pepper

Rinse the quail, pat them dry, and then quarter them, removing the backbones and reserving them for the stock. Set the quail meat aside.

Pour the chicken stock into a small saucepan, add the quail backbones, bring to a simmer, and cook for about 30 minutes. Remove from the heat, strain, and set the stock aside.

Preheat the oven to 350 degrees.

In a Dutch oven or other heavy pot, brown the bacon over medium-high heat until crisp, about 5 minutes. Transfer to absorbent paper to drain. Add the quail pieces to the bacon drippings in the pot and brown on all sides over medium-high heat, about 5 minutes. Transfer to a plate and set aside.

Add the onion, carrots, celery, and garlic to the pot and sauté over medium-high heat, stirring frequently, until browned, about 5 minutes. Add the mushrooms and cook for another 5 minutes. Sprinkle the vegetables with the flour and stir for 1 to 2 minutes until the flour is absorbed.

Add the wine and reserved stock to the pot and cook, stirring often, until the sauce thickens. Reduce the heat and add 1½ tablespoons of the parsley and all of the jelly, brown sugar, and thyme. Season with salt and pepper.

Return the quail and bacon to the pot, cover, place in the oven, and cook until the quail are tender, 30 or 40 minutes.

Serve the ragout hot, garnished with the remaining 1½ tablespoons parsley.

Gazpacho Salad

When the celebrated Japanese cooking instructor Shizuo Tsuji visited Mary Frances at Last House, she wanted to begin the meal with gazpacho. But instead she used the traditional ingredients of the cold summer soup to make a cool, refreshing molded salad. And in place of the bread crumbs she liked to sprinkle on the soup, she served "toasted crusts." *Serves 6*

2 tablespoons unflavored gelatin

3 cups canned tomato juice or tomato-based vegetable juice

1 cup beef consommé

Juice of 1 lemon

Salt

Freshly ground black pepper

1 red sweet bell pepper, peeled, seeded, and diced

2 tomatoes, peeled, seeded, and diced

1 sweet red onion, chopped

1 cucumber, peeled, halved lengthwise, seeded, and diced

Handful of minced fresh herbs such as chives, chervil, parsley, and basil

DRESSING

1 clove garlic

½ cup olive oil

Salt

Freshly ground black pepper

6 thin slices sourdough bread, toasted and buttered

In a small bowl, sprinkle the gelatin over ½ cup of the tomato juice and let stand for 5 minutes to soften. In a saucepan, combine the remaining 2½ cups tomato juice and the consommé and bring to a boil. Remove from the heat and stir in the gelatin mixture until dissolved. Stir in half of the lemon juice and season to taste with salt and pepper. Pour into a 5- or 6-cup ring or loaf mold. Chill until the mixture begins to set.

Fold in the red pepper, tomatoes, onion, cucumber, and herbs, return to the refrigerator, and chill until firm, 4 to 5 hours.

To make the dressing: in a small bowl, mash the garlic in the olive oil to make a paste. Stir in the remaining lemon juice. Salt and pepper to taste.

To unmold, dip the mold briefly (no more than a few seconds) into a pan of hot water, invert a serving plate over the top, and then invert the mold and plate together, giving the mold a good shake. The salad should release smoothly onto the plate. Cut into slices, and top each serving a spoonful of dressing. Accompany with the toasted bread.

Glazed Nuts

Mary Frances had definite ideas about the various elements of a meal, including its preamble. As luncheon or dinner guests arrived and began exchanging pleasantries, she would typically offer them nuts and glasses of chilled white wine. At the very least, she toasted the nuts; optimally, she glazed them, using the following recipe. *Makes 3 cups*

1 teaspoon salt, plus more for seasoning
1 teaspoon sugar
1 teaspoon whole milk
1 teaspoon water
1 egg white
3 cups pecan halves or whole almonds

Preheat the oven to 250 degrees. Line a baking sheet with aluminum foil.

In a small bowl, stir together the 1 teaspoon salt and the sugar, milk, and water.

In a large bowl, beat the egg white using a whisk until stiff peaks form. Fold in the milk mixture just until combined. Stir in the nuts.

Spread the nut mixture on the baking sheet. Bake, stirring every 15 minutes, until the nuts are glazed, about 1 hour.

Remove from oven and season to taste with salt. Serve warm.

IX

The Lodestar

1981–1992

The reprinting of Mary Frances's earlier books, which North Point Press undertook in 1981, greatly expanded her readership beyond the loyal cult of devotees who had followed her every word. And Alfred P. Knopf published two new books, *As They Were* in 1982 and *Sister Age* in 1983, that collected pieces that had been written over the previous thirty years. Reviewers and food journalists began to describe her as "the doyenne of modern gastronomic writing" or a "living national treasure," and they never failed to quote W. H. Auden, who called Mary Frances the "best prose writer in America." Editors of the growing number of culinary magazines sought Mary Frances's opinions on everything from TV dinners to frozen peas, Big Macs, and California cuisine. Professional associates and friends such as James Beard, Julia Child, Simone Beck, Craig Claiborne, Judith Jones, Robert Mondavi, and Alice Waters also lent their names to testimonials and often introduced culinary hopefuls to the woman David Bouverie called his "resident recluse."

In ever increasing numbers, fans, journalists, culinary arrivistes, and aspiring biographers sought out the legendary M. F. K. Fisher. If she was reclusive, she was also hospitable. She answered phone calls herself, and her door was open: the round table set, the wine poured, the larder and refrigerator stocked with dishes proffered by previous visitors or prepared by Mary Frances in the cool early-morning hours—dishes such as a tureen of oyster stew, marinated leeks, celery, and zucchini, or baked mustard-coated chicken thighs. Old friends from St. Helena mingled with relatives who had dropped by, and interviewers and neighbors sat together around the table. Mary Frances herself dined sparingly, but no doubt she remembered the satisfaction she had felt when she served meals in her first kitchen in Dijon, shaking her guests from their "meat-potatoes-gravy" routines.

Mary Frances translated into a California idiom the elaborate rituals she had once questioned in Madame Lanes's dining room in Aix. She served wine in a stemmed glass, used cloth napkins, and insisted that a separate bread plate and knife be at every place setting. When a helpful guest set the table but omitted an essential knife, fork, or spoon, she was uncomfortable and supplied the piece herself. She had made a lifelong practice of dignifying human hungers, and the kitchen was the setting for the transformation.

In a sense, Mary Frances's search for an "ideal" kitchen—her lodestar—began with the dark and dismal kitchen in her family's first Whittier house, a kitchen that was totally separated from the place where food was enjoyed in the dining room. Although the kitchen at the Ranch in Whittier was brighter and was the site of some of Mary Frances's early cooking experiments, this kitchen too was set apart from the dining scene. Her first kitchen on the rue Monge in Dijon intruded into the main room, but the space was minimal, providing an opportunity to cook only simple meals. Although a separate room, the kitchen at Le Paquis was but a few steps from the living room, and guests came into the kitchen to serve themselves from the buffet as well as the stove.

By the Franklin stove, Last House, 1980s. Photograph by Paul Harris.

Over the course of her lifetime, however, Mary Frances gradually combined the spaces for cooking and eating. "The days of hired slaveys and chefs were over," she wrote. "So we began to cook and eat and talk in the same room, and some people still do." The kitchen in St Helena, with its elongated table, also functioned as a dining room and was the focal point for Mary Frances's hospitality. At Last House, she dispensed with kitchen walls altogether, and the kitchen became an integral part of the living and dining room, with still-life arrangements of vegetables and fruits pleasing the eyes.

Hers was a cooking style that involved all the senses. "I believe that through touch, or perhaps because of its agents, other senses regain their first strengths." If initially the sticky and slippery feel of gluey bread dough feels less than pleasing to the novice baker, it helps to appreciate

In the kitchen, Last House, 1980s. Photograph by Paul Harris.

the friendly textures of the satin of a fresh mushroom and the velvet of a peach. At various times she wrote: "Deep bells sound very softly when I see the [avocado] or taste it. . . . I can taste-smell-hear-see and then feel between my teeth the potato chips I ate slowly one November afternoon in 1936, in the bar of the Lausanne Palace. . . . One does not need to be a king or a mogul to indulge most, if not all, of his senses with the heady enjoyment of a dish—speaking in culinary terms that is."

The meals she most savored herself and enjoyed serving forth to her guests were more than mere collections of gastronomical pride and prejudice. Hers was a cuisine based on an extensive knowledge of culinary history, on an informal education in French culinary techniques, on California's abundance, and on sophisticated knavery. She had the confidence to consult Escoffier and to adapt his motto, *"faites simple,"* to her own way of cooking. Experience told her to triple the ginger in the *Joy of Cooking* recipe for gingersnaps, and to take Julia Child to task for the "not doable" recipe for corned beef she had published in a *Parade* article. With a sure palate she went her own way, using such unfashionable ingredients as Bisquick, canned tomato soup, and iceberg lettuce when necessary. In summer, she preferred lightly pickled cucumbers, or cel- ery, snow peas, and peppers dressed with olive oil, lemon juice, and fresh herbs; in winter she ate sweated leeks, zucchini, and peppers marinated in olive oil. Her desserts were fruits served in their own jellies and a home-baked cookie or two. It was all so simple that she often asked, "How can you write about such a tenuous thing?"

In her refusal to be labeled a food journalist or cookbook author, and in her insistence on the pleasures of the table, she stood apart from the home economists who preceded her and were her contemporaries in the 1940s and 1950s, and from many of the writers who have published cook- books during the past fifty years. Part of the reason for this was the value that she placed on the simple, good American food she ate during the first twenty years of her life—"Lots of good food, milk, and fresh vegetables. Always had good cows and I was very fortunate."

She had also experienced years of living in France and Switzerland, and the perspective she gained abroad was enhanced by the ardors and ordeals of cooking in several European kitchens and dining in well- known country inns as well as high-style restaurants and hotels. In France, particularly, she found a definition of food that was based on the fields, forests, vineyards, and seas. The farmers, fishermen, cheese makers, winemakers, and bakers ate what they grew and produced in addition to selling their products to others. And when she cooked with those products, she learned to use a light touch, because there was no need to mask the ingredients, only to enhance them.

Unlike many other Americans who had discovered the glories of French cuisine, Mary Frances never attended formal cooking classes (in fact, she had refused lessons from her landlady, Madame Rigoulot), and she never thought of herself as a recipe developer, a teacher, or an interpreter of Escoffier. Rather, she fell in love with the gastronome Jean Anthelme Brillat-Savarin, and she firmly believed that no recipe had ever "sprung virgin" from her brain. She could read a recipe and find it wanting, unclear, absurd, or amusing. "By now I understand most of the basic principles of cooking in the same way I know how to drive a car, almost by osmosis," she wrote. More often than not, she prepared food without recipes, because "no recipe in the world is independent of the tides, the moon, the physical and emotional temperatures surrounding its performance."

"Of course cooking is a kind of ego trip for me," she told an interviewer. "I don't want compliments at all. But I like to observe, to sense, that the dishes I've made with pattern and deliberation have met their marks." A sly cook but not an accidental one, Mary Frances understood how a simple meal satisfies hunger, how a soufflé arouses a lover, how a crisp potato chip evokes the past, and how Beluga caviar and iced gin produce the ultimate tingling sensation.

Even during the three months of hospice care that preceded Mary Frances's death on June 22, 1992, a raw oyster on the half shell, a forkful of pâté, or a sip of wine brought a smile of satisfaction to her face. The ultimate sensualist, she played the role of "the gastronomical me" to the end. "The stove, the bins, the cupboards made an inviolable throne room. From them I ruled . . . and I loved that feeling."

Minestrone
Adapted from *House Beautiful*

To accommodate some of the aging visitors at Last House, Mary Frances frequently served two or three mugs of different soups as a main course. One of her favorites was minestrone. In *How to Cook a Wolf* she wrote, "Onions, garlic, potatoes, and young cabbage are almost always in the market or your own vegetable bins, and any other vegetables in season may be added with impunity. . . . [Minestrone is] probably the most satisfying soup in the world for people who are hungry, as well as those who are tired or worried or cross or in debt or in a moderate amount of pain or in love or in robust health or in any kind of business huggermuggery." This recipe is as unusual for its consistency as it is for the option of serving it chilled, mixed with sour cream. *Serves 6*

6 cups beef or vegetable stock
8 large waxy potatoes, peeled and quartered
8 carrots, peeled and cut into chunks
3 onions, quartered
8 stalks celery with leaves, cut into 1-inch pieces
½ small head Savoy cabbage, cored and quartered lengthwise
1 small bunch parsley, coarsely chopped
3 cloves garlic, minced
¼ cup olive oil
2 tablespoons tomato paste
Salt
Freshly ground black pepper
Pesto or grated Parmesan cheese for garnish, if serving hot
Sour cream, if serving chilled

In a medium stockpot, bring the stock to a boil and add the potatoes, carrots, onions, celery, cabbage, parsley, and garlic. Reduce the heat to low, cover, and simmer for 1 hour or until the vegetables are soft. Uncover, add the oil and tomato paste, re-cover, and continue to simmer for ½ hour longer. Remove from the heat and mash well with a potato masher to create a coarse puree. Season to taste with salt and pepper.

To serve hot, ladle into bowls and top with a large tablespoon of pesto or Parmesan cheese. Or mash and season as directed, then let cool, mix with 2 to 3 tablespoons sour cream, refrigerate, and serve cold.

Braised Endives in Vinaigrette Sauce

"There are many ways to love a vegetable," Mary Frances wrote in *How to Cook a Wolf*, and she considered cooking a vegetable judiciously an art. Often choosing a vegetable soup or salad rather than meat as a main course, she pared, peeled, lightly cooked, tossed, and served vegetables with great panache. And as she grew older and entertained more frequently, she regularly braised celery stalks or endives, dressed them with a simple vinaigrette, and made them the centerpiece of a light lunch that also included local cheese, sourdough bread, and wine. *Serves 6*

VINAIGRETTE SAUCE

2 teaspoons salt

1 teaspoon freshly ground black pepper

3 tablespoons good-quality vinegar

1 cup olive oil

2 tablespoons drained capers, finely chopped

2 tablespoons finely chopped green onions, including tender
   green parts

½ teaspoon curry powder, 1 teaspoon dry mustard, or 1 tablespoon
   minced fresh parsley or chives (optional)

ENDIVES

1 tablespoon butter, at room temperature

12 Belgian endives, trimmed, rinsed, and patted dry

1 cup vegetable or chicken stock

Salt

Freshly ground black pepper

To make the vinaigrette: combine the salt, pepper, vinegar, oil, capers, green onions, and curry powder (if using) in a glass jar, cover tightly, and shake well to emulsify. Or combine the ingredients in a blender and process until emulsified.

Preheat the oven to 325 degrees.

To prepare the endives: use some of the butter to butter a shallow baking dish large enough to accommodate the endives in a single layer, and arrange the endives in the dish. In a small saucepan, bring the stock to a boil, and pour it over the endives. Season with salt and pepper.

Smear the remaining butter on one side of a sheet of waxed paper and place it, buttered side down, over the endives. Braise in the oven until tender, about 35 minutes.

Remove from the oven and, with a slotted spoon, transfer the endives to a shallow dish. Reserve the stock for another use. (At this point, the endives can be cooled, covered, and refrigerated overnight. Bring to room temperature before continuing.)

Pour the vinaigrette evenly over the endives and let marinate for 2 to 4 hours before serving. To serve, place 2 endives on each plate.

Cantuccini

Adapted from *House Beautiful*

These Tuscan almond cookies look like baked slices from a larger cake, which they more or less are. When her meals grew simpler at Last House, Mary Frances liked to serve these "little Florentine cakes" with fresh fruit or with glasses of *vin santo* for dipping. *Makes about 30*

2½ cups flour

1 teaspoon baking powder

1 cup sugar

¼ teaspoon salt

5 eggs, lightly beaten

½ cup butter, melted

1 cup sliced natural almonds

½ teaspoon aniseeds

Preheat the oven to 350 degrees.

In a bowl, stir together the flour, baking powder, sugar, and salt. Stir in the eggs and then gradually stir in the butter until a dough forms. Add the almonds and aniseeds and knead into dough.

Spread the dough thinly in a buttered 10 × 6-inch glass baking dish, and bake until the dough is set and beginning to turn pale gold around the edges, about 25 minutes. Remove to a rack and cool. Reduce the oven to warm.

Slice into bars about 3 inches long and 1 inch wide. Place the bars, cut side up, on a baking sheet, and dry out in a warm oven for about 10 minutes. Transfer to a wire rack and let cool completely.

Notes

FOREWORD

p. ix   *Peel them gently*   M. F. K. Fisher, *Serve It Forth,* in *The Art of Eating* (New Jersey: Wiley Publishing Company, 2004), 27–28.

p. xi   *what you can cook on a stove*   Elizabeth David, *Is There a Nutmeg in the House?* (New York: Viking, 2001), 3, 5.

p. xii   *unfashionably simple and good*   Anna [Anne] Parrish, "Thoughts about M. F. K. Fisher and Her Work," in *The Art of Eating,* xxiv.

p. xii   *It was the first real day-to-day*   M. F. K. Fisher, *The Gastronomical Me,* in *The Art of Eating,* 438–39.

p. xii   *food respects confidence*   Anthony Bourdain, *Anthony Bourdain's Les Halles Cookbook* (New York: Bloomsbury, 2004), 24.

INTRODUCTION

p. 2   *there is one place*   Amanda Hesser, "Thoughts about M. F. K. Fisher and Her Work," in *The Art of Eating,* xxi.

p. 2   *Anything can be a lodestar*   M. F. K. Fisher, *As They Were* (New York: Alfred A. Knopf, 1982), 89.

p. 3   *A kitchen, the kitchen*   M. F. K. Fisher, "When the Kitchen," *Ford Times*, February 1984, 20.

p. 6   *birds in a tree*   M. F. K. Fisher, *Serve It Forth* (San Francisco: North Point Press, 1989), 5.

p. 6   *When we began cooking these recipes*   Ruth Reichl, "M. F. K. Fisher: A Life in Food," *Los Angeles Times*, June 1991, H1.

p. 7   *There is a communion of more than our bodies*   M. F. K. Fisher, foreword to *The Gastronomical Me* (San Francisco: North Point Press, 1989), x.

CHAPTER 1

p. 11   *The first thing I remember tasting*   *The Gastronomical Me*, 3.

p. 13   *panes of colored crystal*   M. F. K. Fisher, *Among Friends* (New York: Alfred A. Knopf, 1970), 37.

p. 13   *the brown subtle liquid*   Ibid., 50–51.

p. 15   *I decided at the age of nine*   M. F. K. Fisher, "The Best Way to Entertain," *Holiday* (March 1956): 142.

p. 17   *Best of all, we talked-laughed-sang-kissed*   Ibid., 61.

p. 22   *before a bowl of cold white grains of rice*   M. F. K. Fisher, *With Bold Knife and Fork* (New York: Putnam, 1968), 95.

p. 23   *cold thick cream over the hot delights*   Ibid., 273.

p. 23   *The stove, the bins, the cupboards*   *The Gastronomical Me*, 18.

CHAPTER 2

p. 33   *the best institutional food in America*   *The Gastronomical Me*, 21.

p. 39   *interested in dating*   M.F.K. Fisher, "Reminiscences," *Occidental College: Fifty Year Club News* (Winter 1985–86).

p. 40   *I know I shall never taste one*   M.F.K. Fisher, *Consider the Oyster*, in *The Art of Eating*, 166.

CHAPTER 3

p. 42   *I picked up a last delicious crust-crumb*   M.F.K. Fisher, "The Most Important Meal I Ever Ate," *Napa Valley Tables* (Spring/summer 1990), 12.

p. 44   *a kind of avaricious genius*   *The Gastronomical Me*, 65.

p. 45   *this poor wracked harried creature*   M.F.K. Fisher, *Long Ago in France* (New York: Prentice Hall Press, 1991), 133–34.

p. 48   *There in Dijon, the cauliflowers were small*   *The Gastronomical Me*, 103.

p. 49   *shake [her guests] from their routines*   *The Gastronomical Me*, 101.

p. 49   *a complete lack of caution*   M.F.K. Fisher, *An Alphabet for Gourmets* (San Francisco: North Point Press, 1989), 17.

p. 49   *Instead of curtains, I would have Venetian blinds*   *Serve It Forth*, 126.

p. 53   *about eating and about what to eat*   *Serve It Forth*, 4.

p. 54   *I drink to our pasts*   *Serve It Forth*, 81.

CHAPTER 4

p. 67   *But what really mattered*   *An Alphabet for Gourmets*, 165–66.

p. 73   *The world seeped in*   *The Gastronomical Me*, 209.

CHAPTER 5

p. 81   *I remember that I wrote a sad little criticism*   M. F. K. Fisher, *Dubious Honors* (San Francisco: North Point Press, 1988), 135.

p. 83   *balance is something that depends entirely on the individual*   M. F. K. Fisher, *How to Cook a Wolf* (San Francisco: North Point Press, 1988), 4.

p. 83   *an enormous salad*   Ibid., 9.

p. 83   *A smoother, thicker, richer soup*   Ibid., 135.

p. 84   *It seemed quite natural to do a good book*   *Dubious Honors*, 136.

p. 86   *I telephoned the restaurant*   *An Alphabet for Gourmets*, 25–27.

p. 90   *I myself was a fascinated witness*   Ibid., 66.

p. 90   *twice as delicious, if that were possible*   Donald Friede, "On Being Married to M. F. K. Fisher," *Gastronomica* (Winter 2002): 76.

p. 92   *A writing cook and a cooking writer*   *With Bold Knife and Fork*, 173.

CHAPTER 6

p. 100   *I think of myself dining*   *An Alphabet for Gourmets*, 210.

p. 103   *the green tunnel of the Cours*   M. F. K. Fisher, *Map of Another Town* (Boston: Little Brown, 1964), 34.

p. 107   *One can't eat that way*   M. F. K. Fisher, interview with author, June 1987.

p. 108   *running down our hill*   Quoted in Joan Zoloth, "M. F. K. Fisher and Me," *Diablo* (November 1999): 24.

p. 112   *simple, unfashionably simple and good*   *The Art of Eating,* xxiv.

p. 116   *my children would be waiting for me*   *Map of Another Town,* 273.

p. 118   *Most people, especially men*   *With Bold Knife and Fork,* 58.

CHAPTER 7

p. 132   *trying to run an unlicensed*   *As They Were,* 258.

CHAPTER 8

p. 139   *a guest in a delightful rented cottage*   *As They Were,* 259.

p. 140   *The one in Marseille*   Ibid., 89.

p. 140   *We had perhaps four pans and kettles*   Ibid., 92.

p. 145   *It is very simple*   Ibid., 251.

CHAPTER 9

p. 153   *The days of hired slaveys*   "When the Kitchen," 21.

p. 153   *I believe that through touch*   M. F. K. Fisher, "Learn to Touch . . . to Smell . . . to Taste," *Vogue,* March 1972, 116.

p. 154   *Deep bells sound very softly*   *With Bold Knife and Fork,* 44, 101.

p. 155   *Lots of good food*   Joan Nathan, "A Conversation with M. F. K. Fisher," *Washington Post,* August 24, 1986, 16.

p. 156   *By now I understand*   *With Bold Knife and Fork*, 115.

p. 156   *no recipe in the world*   *How to Cook a Wolf*, 100.

p. 156   *Of course cooking is a kind of ego trip*   M. F. K. Fisher, interview with author, June 1987.

p. 156   *The stove, the bins, the cupboards*   *The Gastronomical Me*, 18.

p. 157   *Onions, garlic, potatoes, and young cabbage*   *How to Cook a Wolf*, 39.

p. 159   *There are many ways to love a vegetable*   *How to Cook a Wolf*, 137.

California Studies in Food and Culture

Darra Goldstein, Editor

•

DESIGNER: SANDY DROOKER

TEXT: 10.5/15 FILOSOFIA

DISPLAY: FILOSOFIA

COMPOSITOR: INTEGRATED COMPOSITION SYSTEMS

ILLUSTRATOR: AVRAM DUMITRESCU

PRINTER/BINDER: FRIESENS CORPORATION